Cambridge Elements ≡

Elements in Contentious Politics
edited by
David S. Meyer
University of California, Irvine
Suzanne Staggenborg
University of Pittsburgh

T0311486

LAW, MOBILIZATION, AND SOCIAL MOVEMENTS

How Many Masters?

Whitney K. Taylor
San Francisco State University

Sidney Tarrow
Cornell University

CAMBRIDGE
UNIVERSITY PRESS

Shaftesbury Road, Cambridge CB2 8EA, United Kingdom

One Liberty Plaza, 20th Floor, New York, NY 10006, USA

477 Williamstown Road, Port Melbourne, VIC 3207, Australia

314–321, 3rd Floor, Plot 3, Splendor Forum, Jasola District Centre, New Delhi – 110025, India

103 Penang Road, #05–06/07, Visioncrest Commercial, Singapore 238467

Cambridge University Press is part of Cambridge University Press & Assessment, a department of the University of Cambridge.

We share the University's mission to contribute to society through the pursuit of education, learning and research at the highest international levels of excellence.

www.cambridge.org
Information on this title: www.cambridge.org/9781009493017

DOI: 10.1017/9781009493024

© Whitney K. Taylor and Sidney Tarrow 2024

This publication is in copyright. Subject to statutory exception and to the provisions of relevant collective licensing agreements, no reproduction of any part may take place without the written permission of Cambridge University Press & Assessment.

When citing this work, please include a reference to the DOI 10.1017/9781009493024

First published 2024

A catalogue record for this publication is available from the British Library.

ISBN 978-1-009-49301-7 Hardback
ISBN 978-1-009-49300-0 Paperback
ISSN 2633-3570 (online)
ISSN 2633-3562 (print)

Cambridge University Press & Assessment has no responsibility for the persistence or accuracy of URLs for external or third-party internet websites referred to in this publication and does not guarantee that any content on such websites is, or will remain, accurate or appropriate.

Law, Mobilization, and Social Movements

How Many Masters?

Elements in Contentious Politics

DOI: 10.1017/9781009493024
First published online: February 2024

Whitney K. Taylor
San Francisco State University

Sidney Tarrow
Cornell University

Author for correspondence: Whitney K. Taylor, wktaylor@sfsu.edu

Abstract: Legal and social movement scholars have long puzzled over the role of movements in moving, being moved by, and changing the meanings of the law. But for decades, these two strands of scholarship only dovetailed at their edges, in the work of a few far-seeing scholars. The fields began to more productively merge before and after the turn of the century. In this Element, the authors take an interactive approach to this problem and sketch four mechanisms that seem promising in effecting a true fusion: legal mobilization, legal-political opportunity structure, social construction, and movement–countermovement interaction. The Element also illustrates the workings and interactions of these four mechanisms from two examples of the authors' work: the campaign for same-sex marriage in the United States and social constitutionalism in South Africa.

Keywords: social movements, law, legal mobilization, same-sex marriage, social constitutionalism

ISBNs: 9781009493017 (HB), 9781009493000 (PB), 9781009493024 (OC)
ISSNs: 2633-3570 (online), 2633-3562 (print)

Contents

Introduction

Two decades after the Supreme Court's decision in *Brown* v. *Board of Education*,[1] the late Civil Rights attorney and Harvard law professor, Derrick Bell Jr., published a widely cited article, "Serving Two Masters" (Bell 1976). Bell worried that dissent was growing between civil rights lawyers and African American communities on the strategy of seeking equality through school integration. As he wrote in the introduction to his article:

> Having achieved so much by courageous persistence, they [e.g., civil rights lawyers] have not wavered in their determination to implement *Brown* using racial balance measures developed in the hard-fought legal battles of the last two decades. This stance involves great risk for clients whose educational interests may no longer accord with the integration ideals of their attorneys . . . .there is tardy concern that racial balance may not be the relief actually desired by the victims of segregated schools.

"It is difficult," Bell warned, "to provide standards for the attorney and protection for the client where the source of the conflict is the attorney's ideals" (471–2). Quoting the Book of Luke, he concluded; "*No servant can serve two masters:* for either he will hate the one and love the other; or else he will hold to one, and despise the other" (Luke 16: 18, King James).

"In acknowledging the influence of class interest and donor pressure on lawyer goals and tactics," writes Doug NeJaime (2012: 666), "Bell was the first to expose the tensions inherent in cause lawyers' representation of large, diverse groups." But Bell never specified the role of the *social movement* of which the Legal Defense Fund was a part and which developed in the context of the structural changes brought on by the war and depression.[2] Nor did he explicate the interactions among the lawyers who pled their cases, the constituents they represented, the broader movement of which both were a part, and the institutions before which they made their claims. It is these multiple interactions – and the mechanisms that drive them – that form the core of this Element. In what follows, we advance an interactive approach to this problem and sketch four mechanisms that seem to us promising in effecting a true fusion: *legal mobilization, legal-political opportunity structure, social construction,* and *movement-countermovement interaction.*

---

[1] 347 US 483 (1954).

[2] See the definition of movements in Tarrow (2022: 11) as "collective challenges based on common purposes and social solidarities, in sustained interaction with elites, opponents, and authorities." On the impact of the depression and the Second World War on African Americans, see Doug McAdam, *The Political Process and the Development of Black Insurgency, 1930–1970* (1982 [1999]).

In the decades after Bell published his critique, social movements were increasingly recognized by legal scholars as intervening actors in the relations between courts and claimants. As Jack Balkin and Reva Siegel noted in a 2006 essay, "Social Movements continuously integrate law and the institutions of civil society" (946). But for a long time, legal scholars failed to develop much expertise what was happening in social movement scholarship that might have helped them to integrate the two fields of study. For example, in their essay, Balkin and Siegel did not cite any social movement theorists, despite the considerable overlaps between their theory and the advances in social movement research in the decades when they were writing.

Conversely, few movement scholars paid sufficient attention to the interactions between movements and the law, even though they were aware that many movements' claims ended up in the courts. Even after they began to do so, they tended to posit a one-way causal relationship between law and movements, eliding the interactions among the courts, movements, and the constituencies they worked to represent. Apart from a few exceptions (Handler 1978; Klare 1978; Barkan 1980, 1985; Zemans 1983), there were few examples of "crossover work" that could foster a junction between these two flourishing fields.

In this Element, we follow the progress of the crossover work that developed within both specialties on both sides of the turn of the century before presenting our own theory, in which we investigate the interactions among lawyers, movement organizations, key constituencies, and institutions. We present a detailed – though not comprehensive – survey of social movement scholarship and legal scholarship, as well as this crossover work. In the process, we attempt to draw on a wide range of scholars, who focus on different issue areas and different areas of the world. For scholars who are conversant in both this historical development and recent works in these traditions, the first few parts of this Element will be largely familiar. In the latter parts of the Element, we present a new approach to best effect the fusion of law and social movement scholarship – these sections will be novel, even to those most up-to-date on these literatures. We offer both this detailed survey and our new approach with the hope that this Element will be useful to future generations of scholars, as well as those already steeped in the fields of law and social movements.

This Element proceeds as follows: In Section 1, we show why social movement scholars have been slow to integrate the law into their empirical approaches. In Section 2, we focus on three streams of legal scholarship: first, on "rights-based" analyses and on the critique of rights that followed in what came to be called "critical legal studies"; second, the literature on "cause lawyering"; and, third, the strand of scholarship that we summarize with the term "popular constitutionalism."

Section 3 turns to the growing "crossover" tradition, across both issue areas and different areas of the world. Beginning from the debate between Gerald Rosenberg (1991) and McCann (1994), we will show that a broader conception of the law – one that reaches well beyond the courts – has helped to make movements more accessible to legal scholars, but has been less satisfactory in specifying the mechanisms through which lawyers and movements intersect.

In Section 4, we lay out our own theory for integrating social movement theory and socio-legal studies. We build on four mechanisms that we hope will advance the fusion between these two traditions:

- *First, legal mobilization*: the efforts of social movements to use and expand the law to advance their claims;
- *Second, the social construction of the law* which has enabled movement activists to advance their claims;
- *Third, political and legal opportunity structure*, concepts that surround and constrain efforts at legal mobilization;
- *Fourth,* the process of *movement-countermovement interaction,* both in and outside the courts, which produces outcomes of legal mobilization that are often quite different than what movements intend.

In Section 5, drawing on our own research, we integrate these traditions: first, in the conflict over same sex marriage in the United States; and then on the impact of social constitutionalism in South Africa. The Element concludes with a series of questions that we hope will mark the next generation of legal/social movement scholarship.

Why Do We Care?

Why does it seem important to advance this scholarly integration? In crafting this essay, we have had three motivations:

First, more knowledge is always better than less; we think exposing the work of scholars in each of the traditions to scholars in other is itself a worthy aim;[3]

Second, the "fields" in which movements and the law come together are of particular importance for public policy and constitutional development, especially in this era of rising inequality and polarization. We hope our efforts will make contributions to both of these areas;

---

[3] Once again, we do not claim to be alone. In 2006, Michael McCann put together an exhaustive reader called *Law and Social Movements*. More recently, in 2023, Steven Boutcher, Corey Shdaimah, and Michael Yarbrough have put together a mammoth *Handbook on Law, Movements, and Social Change*, which includes a great deal of work coming from outside the United States.

Finally, we hope that the interactive theory that we put forward in Section 4 and illustrate in Section 5 of this Element will serve as a model for the efforts of other scholars working to fuse social movement and legal perspectives in these areas of research and practice.

1 How Movement Scholars Turned to the Law

In this section, we briefly show how and why social movement scholars since the 1960s turned toward the law but why empirical, theoretical, and methodological elements in the budding social movement field left a void between this field of scholarship and parallel advances in socio-legal studies until quite recently.

1.1 The Sources of the Turn in Social Movement-Scholarship

The modern field of social movement studies grew out of three main roots, which came together in the early 1960s: *collective behavior, structural Marxism, and historical sociology.*[4] While these sources differed in many ways, what they had in common was seeing social movements as only one of a number of forms of collective action. Movements were variously seen as parts of unorganized collective action (the collective behavior approach); the development of conflicts triggered by modern capitalism (structural Marxism); and conflicts accompanying the rise of the modern state (historical sociology).

Influenced by the horrifying outcome of Europe's interwar movements and the horrors to which they led, early postwar movement scholars argued that mass demonstrations undermine the rule of law and threaten democracy. The civil rights and student movements showed that movement activists were just as intelligent, well schooled, psychologically normal, and instrumental as other people (Keniston 1960). In the words of former activists and distinguished movement scholars Frances Piven and Richard Cloward (1992), this move served to "normalize" protest. The crystallization of a distinct field of social movement studies attached to politics helped scholars to better understand the extraordinary surge of contentious collective action over the last half-century, with tools that were based on the assumption that movements were "normal" and constituted noninstitutional forms of participation in more-or-less structured relations to institutional politics (McAdam 1982; Meyer and Staggenborg 1996, 2022; Tarrow 2012). These scholars came to define social movements as "collective challenges, based on common purposes and social solidarities, in

---

[4] For a telescopic outline of these classical sources and their role in social movement studies, see McAdam and Tarrow (2019).

sustained interaction with elites, opponents, and authorities" (Tarrow 2011: 9), a definition that we adopt throughout this Element.

1.2 The Effects of Normalization

The normalization of movements had both a negative and a positive aspect: on the negative side, it led many scholars to dismiss traditional movements, like the labor movement, as "old" social movements (Offe 1985)[5]; on the positive side, it led scholars to pay more attention to the connections between the law and social movements. In the forefront of this move were young scholars like Steven Boutcher – both writing on his own (2010) and with collaborators (Boutcher and Stobaugh 2013; Boutcher and McCammon 2019), Epp (1998), Gianluca de Fazio (2012), Hilson (2002), McCammon (2012), McCann (1994), Polletta (2000), Gerald Rosenberg (1991), and Vanhala (2010).

There were aspects of the new social movement scholarship that continued to retard its fusion with legal scholarship, however: the advent of widespread – and almost obsessive – employment of survey methods; a preoccupation with movement organizations; and the development of movement scholars' most original contribution to the social sciences: protest event analysis. Although all three were major innovations, they dovetailed imperfectly with the methods and the objectives of legal scholarship.

1.2.1 Surveying Social Movements

When legal scholars analyze reform-minded legal cases, they turn naturally to the case method, because the law proceeds through cases, especially in common law systems like the American one. But as social movement scholars struggled for recognition in the social sciences, they adopted methodologies that would legitimate movements as a valid field of political participation, and these were mainly quantitative, and not case-oriented.

The first adaptation was the use of survey research. In their book *Political Action: Mass Participation in Five Western Democracies*, Samuel Barnes and Max Kaase (1979) employed surveys with citizens to find out what forms of political participation they reported having employed. As expected, there were many more respondents who claimed to have voted or supported candidates than those who engaged in "unconventional political activities" (58). The latter category included everything from writing to a newspaper to damaging property to the use of guns or explosives, passing through signing petitions, occupying

---

[5] Except for isolated research by scholars like Klare (1978–9) in the 1970s, organized labor was largely left out of social movement scholarship after its Cold War-induced de-radicalization.

buildings, and boycotting goods (66). Not surprisingly, the more "unconventional" the form, the less frequent was its reported use.

In an important innovation building on survey research, social movement scholars have recently begun employing surveys to dig more deeply into movement activism. In Europe, Bert Klandermans and Nonna Mayer (2006) employed surveys to analyze activists in far-right movements. In the United States, Christopher Parker and Matt Barreto (2013) used similar methods to understand activism in the Tea Party. Fisher (2019) employed surveys of participants during protest events.

Although these methodological innovations are ingenious and fruitful, their practitioners struggled to gain access into the internal lives of movements or how movement activism intersects with the law (Andretta and della Porta 2014). Survey research can produce pictures of the attitudes of citizens toward political activity in general, but it is difficult to connect these attitudes to on-the-ground or real-world behavior. The problem with using survey methods alone to measure legal consciousness is that closed-ended questions provide little insight into how "people think about and use the law," in part because the nature of the questions, where respondents select from a predetermined list of answers, and in part because surveys capture only a snapshot moment rather than dynamic processes (Merry 1990).

1.2.2 Organizational Analysis

At the same time as survey research was growing as a tool of social scientific analysis, a group of sociologists around Mayer Zald at the University of Michigan began to apply insights from organization theory to the study of movements. Their first move was distinguishing between movements and movement organizations.[6] In contrast to Mancur Olson's microeconomic account, which focused on the problems of effecting collective action (1965), McCarthy and Zald were struck by the great increase in the organization of collective action in America in the 1960s (1973). From this, they derived a theory of what they called "resource mobilization" (1977), which became the basis for a broad rethinking of social movement theory (Davis et al. 2005). The resource mobilization approach considers "resources that must be mobilized," as well as "the linkages of social movements to other groups, the dependence of movements upon external support for success, and the tactics used by authorities to control or incorporate movements," rather than focusing

---

[6] Many of the products of the "resource mobilization" school will be found in Zald and McCarthy (1987).

on levels of deprivation or the beliefs that mobilized actors hold (McCarthy and Zald 1977: 1213).

But to our knowledge, few scholarly efforts were made to connect movement *organizations* to the law: Handler's 1978 book *Social Movements and the Legal System* explicitly drew of resource mobilization theory. Barkan's 1984 article on "Political Trials and Resource Mobilization" stood out as a rare application of McCarthy and Zald's theory to the legal system. And the essay "Law, Organizations, and Social Movements" (2010) by Lauren Edelman, Gwendolyn Leachman, and Doug McAdam is the only effort we have found to employ organization theory in a systematic way to examine the relations between law and movements.

1.2.3 Protest Event Analysis

The most original methodological innovation in social movement scholarship is the systematic study of aggregates of protest events.[7] From the 1970s on, movement scholars began to collect, enumerate and analyze protest event data. In Great Britain (Tilly 1995), Germany (Rucht 1998), Italy (Tarrow 1989), the United States (Jenkins and Perrow 1977; McAdam 1982), and in a range of European countries (Kriesi et al. 1995). Suspicious of the accuracy and the objectivity of official data, they began to systematically mine newspapers and other sources to track the rise and fall of cycles of contention and the forms of protest employed by protesters.

Protest event data added consistency and historicity to the study of how citizens use public forms of collective action. But the quantitative logic of protest event analysis dovetailed poorly with the case-based nature of most legal research. Part of the problem came from the fact that newspaper accounts of protest focused inordinately on the more dramatic or more violent forms of contentious action (McCarthy 1996). But a deeper problem was its focus on participation in public space. Only in 2015, in a landmark article on the relations between movements, high profile rape trials, and policy advocacy did Kristine Coulter and David S. Meyer combine protest event analysis with detailed examination of legal cases.

In summary, by the 1980s, a flourishing field of social movement studies began to detach itself from earlier and less precise notions of collective behavior, structural Marxism, and historical sociology. At its boundary, a few scholars began to reach out to the field of legal studies, but the methodologies of survey research, protest event analysis, and organizational analysis fit in poorly with

---

[7] For a primer on this method, see Hutter (2014).

the case-based approaches of legal scholars, who – in the meantime – were struggling to reach out to social movement studies, as we will see in Section 2.

2 Legal Scholars Turn to Movements

From the 1960s on, legal and socio-legal scholars began to study popular efforts to influence the law, especially in the US context (e.g., Scheingold 1974; Galanter 1974; Handler 1978; Zemans 1983; Olson 1984). The study of "cause lawyers," the kinds of cases they bring to the courts, and the consequences of the turn to law for social change came to preoccupy socio-legal scholars, while scholars working in the legal academy engaged in efforts to forward popular constitutionalism as a normative and empirical theory of law and movement studies. Both sets of scholars owed a debt to studies of "the politics of rights" and to the challenge to the civil rights movement by Derrick Bell and the critical legal studies that followed. But both were hamstrung by the fact that most legal scholars came from the legal academy in which the major question put to students was how to construct a winning case in court. Only around the turn of the century did legal scholars begin to place the relations between law and movements within a broader framework of multidimensional advocacy in which winning a case was only one possible outcome of the interaction of law and movements, picking up on insights developed by earlier socio-legal scholars (NeJaime 2011, 2012). We will turn to these broader outcomes in Section 3, where we begin to show how legal and social movement scholarship began to merge.

2.1 Rights and the Critique of Rights

In his notable book, *The Politics of Rights,* political scientist Scheingold (1974) zeroed in on the overwhelming emphasis on rights that marked the two decades of progressive legal scholarship after *Brown*. In their pure form, as he saw it, rights are a myth. "The myth of rights," Scheingold declared, "rests on a faith in the political efficacy and ethical sufficiency of law as a principle of government. "The myth of rights," he specified, ". . . assures us that the path of the law is consistent with our fundamental political ideals as they are enshrined in various provisions of the Constitution and the Bill of Rights" (17).

Like many who followed in his footsteps, Scheingold saw rights as an *ideology* – a particularly powerful one in the American political tradition, but one that was less a description of reality than a wish for their fulfillment. Rights, he concluded, are *resources,* and are therefore dependent on the power of those who wield them. "The myth of rights," he wrote, "may work on behalf of change, but its dominant tendency is surely to reinforce the status quo" (91). Recalling Bell, he reasoned that "There is no need to look any further than school desegregation problems to realize that the declaration of rights does not purge political conflict of its power dimensions" (85). Going beyond Bell, he concluded pessimistically that "litigation emerges as a strategy of desperation rather than hope" (95).

Scheingold turned to a variable that was absent from Bell's critique – *mobilization* – which gestured toward the social movement field.[8] He described a dual process of *activating* a quiescent citizenry and *organizing* groups into effective political units. Political mobilization can in this fashion build support for interests that have been excluded from existing allocations of values and thus promote a *realignment* of political forces (131). But although his concept of mobilization was remarkably close to the work that Charles Tilly (1979) and other movement scholars were doing at the time, he did not access that tradition or try to build on it. Nor did his concept of mobilization lead him beyond the role of law and courts. On the contrary, he explained, "Insofar as court decisions can legitimate claims and cue expectations, litigation can contribute to both activation and organization; to the building of new coalitions; and, in the long run, to a realignment of forces within the political arena" (Scheingold 1974: 132). Scheingold ended his analysis on a cautious note. "The evidence," he warned, "suggests that litigation may be useful for providing remedies for individuals but . . . its impact on social policy is open to question" (148).

2.2 Critical Legal Studies

About the same time as Scheingold was underscoring "the political of rights," a new strand of theorizing – critical legal studies (CLS) – emerged in the legal academy.[9] Building a critique of the emphasis on rights that had come out of the civil rights movement and of the artificial distinction between law and politics, CLS scholars began to question the role of courts and lawyers as a contributing factor in liberalism's decline. As Scott Cummings (2017b: 1587) put it in a thorough analysis:

> As the legal liberal vision of social change appeared to reach its limit – erupting in bitter fights over abortion, busing, and affirmative action – optimism began to fade. Rather than "balancing the scales of justice," legal liberalism came to

---

[8] It is important that the premier journal of social movement studies in the United States is called *Mobilization,* which was founded in the 1980s.

[9] We cannot hope to summarize the various strands of theories and counter-theories that were part of the Critical Legal Studies movement. A critical perspective is offered by Laura Kalman in her *The Strange Career of Legal Liberalism* (1998). More sympathetic accounts were offered by Morton Horwitz, in *The Transformation of American Law* (1992), by Karl Klare in "Law-Making as Praxis" (1979), by Mark Tushnet in his "Critical Legal Studies: A Political History" (1991), and by Roberto Unger, in *The Critical Legal Studies Movement* (1983). After-the-fact reflections were offered by Duncan Kennedy in his *The Rise and Fall of Classical Legal Thought* (2006), and by Orly Lobel in his "The Paradox of Extralegal Activism" (2007).

> be seen as woefully inadequate to challenge deeply ingrained social
> inequality . . . . At this moment, progressive scholars began to sour on the liberal
> legal project itself – producing a critical turn in analyzing the role of law in
> social change.

Successive generations of CLS scholars applied the methodology to various
forms of hierarchy and subordination, until – from its central trunk of CLS –
more radical perspectives emerged. The liveliest strands of this development
emerged from two important spinoffs: critical feminist theory[10] and critical race
theory.[11] The former, which was deeply influenced by Foucauldian social
theory, had an impact mainly in academia. Critical race theory had the most
significant impact beyond the legal academy, in large part because it was
mischaracterized by right-wing politicians and conflated with the Black Lives
Matter movement.

Remarkably, although critical legal scholars regarded their community as
a movement, it had little concrete connection to the ripening field of social
movement studies. In his reflections on CLS, in fact, Tushnet (1991: 1515)
saw it *not* as a movement but as a "political location," one in which "people
with a wide but not unlimited range of political views can come together for
political education, sustenance, and activity." It was only in the 1990s that
progressive lawyers began to move beyond these internal debates to a broader
concept of "legal mobilization" (McCann 1992: 226). As we will see in
Section 3, it was through this concept that legal scholars began to give
a distinct analytical and organizational space to social movements. The first
stage in this evolution was a series of volumes on what came to be called
"cause lawyering."

2.3 From the Politics of Rights to Cause Lawyering

Across five edited volumes, working with Austin Sarat and various collaborators, Scheingold explored the contours of cause lawyering and, in one volume,
its intersection with social movements.[12] The overwhelming focus of this body

---

[10] For a general analysis of feminist critical theory, see Martha A. Fineman's "Feminism in the
Law: The Difference it Makes" (1992) and *Feminist Legal Theory: A Primer,* edited by Nancy
Levit and Robert Verchick (2nd ed. 2016). For a critical perspective on the turn to Foucauldian
social theory in legal feminism, see Robin West, "Women in the Legal Academy: A Brief History
of Feminist Legal Theory" (2018).

[11] Landmarks in the development of critical race theory were Richard Delgado's and Jean Stefano's
Critical Race Theory: An Introduction (2001) and Kimberlé Crenshaw Williams' "Twenty Years
of Critical Race Theory" (2011). Only in the age of Trump has it been appropriated – and
misappropriated – by the Right for electoral purposes. For an astute journalistic analysis, see
Smith (2021).

[12] These volumes included: *Cause Lawyering: Political Commitments and Professional
Responsibilities* (1997), *Cause Lawyering and the State in a Global Era* (2001), *Something to*

of work was on what cause lawyers do, on their motivations, and on how they differ from traditional or "professional" lawyers. But Sarat and Scheingold (2004: 19) did view cause lawyers and social movements as overlapping entities:

> ...political cause lawyering functions in multiple venues ranging from lobbying through political mobilization and organizations to street demonstrations and civil disobedience . . . Political cause lawyering can also involve participation in social movements – both as movement activists and as attorneys supporting direct political action.

In their edited volume, *Cause Lawyers and Social Movements*, Sarat and Scheingold (2006: 1) focused on what "cause lawyers do *for*, and *to*, social movements." In that volume, they divided the roles of cause lawyers into their defensive and offensive components. In terms of defense, they lawyers "offer preventive assistance by clarifying the boundary between lawful and unlawful disruptions" undertaken by activists during direct action campaigns. "When movement activists cross that boundary," they wrote, "or are deemed to have done so by the authorities, cause lawyers can either mount a conventional defense in hopes of securing an acquittal or they can, ordinarily at the behest of and under instructions from the activists, politicize the trial so as to generate public support for the movement" (9).

In this offensive role, Sarat and Scheingold explain, "the courtroom becomes an arena of movement activism, and cause lawyers, almost by definition, are elevated from support staff to positions of leadership." However, they add, "cause lawyers contribute most compellingly to movements not as the result of the direct consequences of litigation but indirectly through deploying courtroom encounters strategically – irrespective of whether decisions go in their favor" (10).

Much of the ensuing debate on cause lawyering centered on this offensive role, in effect merging with an ongoing debate about the extent to which social change can reasonably be sought through litigation, to which we will turn in Section 3. But Sarat, Scheingold, and their contributors dealt only glancingly with the broader set of issues that were emerging in the growing field of social movements: What does this mean to the general public? How do movement organizations dovetail with lawyering? How do protest events interact with action in the courts? Although their initial focus was on lawyers in the United

---

Believe In: Politics, Professionalism and Cause Lawyering (2004), *The Worlds Cause Lawyers Make: Structure and Agency in Legal Practice* (2005), *Cause Lawyers and Social Movements* (2006), and *The Cultural Lives of Cause Lawyers* (2008). Sarat recognized the unique contribution of his late collaborator in *The Legacy of Stuart Scheingold* (2012).

States, later scholars expanded the geographic focus on studies on cause lawyering (see, e.g., Tam 2013; Arrington 2019a).

The major strength of the cause lawyering tradition was that it helped to distinguish cause lawyers from common-or-garden legal practitioners; its weakness, however, was that its focus on litigation and on lawyers encouraged participants to disregard the interactive relationship between movement organizations, the constituencies they represent, and the law. This broader connection would be taken up between the 1990s and the first two decades of the twenty-first century by a second group of scholars focused on US constitutional law who attempted to forward what we summarize as "popular constitutionalism." While these scholars were most interested in the specifics of the US context, their scholarship significantly influenced the broader field of law and social movements.

2.4 Popular Constitutionalism

As representatives of this tradition, we will focus on four of these authors: two of them – Larry Kramer and Bruce Ackerman – had strong normative commitments to popular constitutionalism; two others – Reva Siegel and Michael Klarman – took more detailed historical and analytical approaches, giving careful attention to the place of particular legal cases in the development of legal jurisprudence and to the intersection between the US Supreme Court and public and movement opinion. Although all four authors gave a prominent place to the Supreme Court, they took bold steps in the direction of broader issues, which took them closer to the social movement tradition. Popular constitutionalism – as we interpret it – reaches beyond the courts to the broader range of citizen groups that interact with the legal system on behalf of social and political claims, and the study of popular constitutionalism in the US offers clear "portable insights" (Simmons 2016) for those working on constitutionalism in other contexts.

2.4.1 Ackerman on We the People

In a series of books beginning in the early 1990s, Bruce Ackerman has seen American constitutional history as part of a cyclical dynamic, specifying a number of tipping points that he regarded as key turning points.[13] These turning points were sometimes marked by formal Article Five amendments – like those that marked the Reconstruction period – but Ackerman insisted that

---

[13] Ackerman's massive contribution appeared in three volumes published over a 14-year period: Vol. I, *We the People: Foundations* (1991), Vol. II, *We the People: Transformations* (2000), and Vol. III, *We the People: The Civil Rights Revolution* (2018).

something like Article Five changes can be identified even in the absence of formal amendments.

Ackerman (2014: 44–6) theorized about how these reversals occurred, charting a multi-stage model of constitutional change based on five successive mechanisms:

- *Signaling*: the first stage in constitutional dynamics in which one or another institution responds to the appeals of one or another reform movement;
- *The proposal phase*, in which the reform movement – now ensconced in the political process – keeps on winning elections and the House, Senate, and the President are prepared to pass landmark statutes;
- *The triggering election*, if and when the movement for revolutionary reform wins big at the polls;
- *Mobilized elaboration*, in which the rising movement is now largely in control of all the key institutions;
- *The consolidating phase and ratifying election*. Creative periods never last: popular support may slacken, and the reformers turn into establishment figures. Surprisingly, in this consolidation, even the opposition moderates its stance to adapt to the new constitutional settlement.

Ackerman is best known among constitutional lawyers for his thesis that revisions of the American Constitution no longer depend on the Article Five amendment process. He links this thesis to a more general critique of what he sees as the unwillingness of constitutional lawyers to look beyond formalism to major changes in the constitutional order that take place outside the courts. For social movement scholars, the most important implication of Ackerman's critique is that non-state actors are more likely to push for constitutional revisions outside Article Five than struggle through the obstacle course of the formal amendment process.

Movement scholars would agree with Ackerman that movements do not empower political change on their own; they transform into or influence what he calls "movement-parties."[14] This transition leads to the "normalization of movement politics," which gives added importance to the election of a movement president and to the plebiscitarian presidency.[15] For example, in the third volume of his trilogy, Ackerman (2014: 41) argues that *Brown* and its progeny initiated a new constitutional model that was superimposed on the New Deal constitution. Following this line of argument, he identifies Lyndon Johnson as a "movement-president" in the line of filiation begun by FDR.

---

[14] On the concept of "movement parties," see Van Cott (2005), Schlozman (2015), and Tarrow (2021).

[15] Ackerman was deeply influenced by his Yale colleague, Steven Skowronek (1997).

Whether or not that is a fair depiction of LBJ, the constitutional changes represented by the Civil Rights period still frame the constitutional debate today.

There are problems in Ackerman's *tour de force,* beginning with the status and specification of the master concept of "The People." For example, does his model involve *all* of the people, *some* of the people, all of the people *some of the time,* or some of them *all of the time*? And how does the term "The People" relate to the more specific term "social movement?" As Levinson (2014: 2672) remarked in his pungent comment on Ackerman's book:

> ...tellingly, for all the invocations of "We the People," *The Civil Rights Revolution* underscores the extent to which Ackerman's historical project, remarkable as it is, focuses on elite leaders and not really on the great unwashed who might have constituted the political base for at least some of these leaders.

While Ackerman's notion of cyclical change followed by normalization is familiar to social movement scholars, there are two main differences: First, while movement scholars have largely limited their attention to cycles of contention *outside* the state with the government as the target of their challenges, Ackerman's constitutional moments take place *within* the state, and, in particular, in the interactions among the executive, Congress, and the courts. Second, while, for movement theorists, the interaction of movements and institutions takes place *throughout the cycle,* in Ackerman's scheme, movements appear only at the inception of the cycle – in what he calls "the signaling stage." The result is that most of the action in Ackerman's cycles takes place within institutional politics, and not in the relations between institutions and movements.

2.4.2 Kramer on The People Themselves

Coming chronologically in the midst of Ackerman's *oeuvre,* Kramer's 2001 forward to the *Harvard Law Review's* "The 2000 Supreme Court Year" and his 2004 book, *The People Themselves,* came close to calling for the displacement of the "counter-majoritarian" Court by the elected branches of government and those they represent. Kramer quotes John Dickinson's *Letters from a Farmer in Pennsylvania,* who asked: "Ought we not watch the people? And have they not a right of JUDGING from the evidence before them, on no slighter points than their *liberty* and *happiness?"* (2004: 312–25). However, the closest Kramer comes to identifying actual social movements in the debates leading up to the revolution is the evidence of the right to vote, to petition, and to organize assemblies and "more assertive forms of resistance, invoked in many instances only after a formal public notice had been issued and a public meeting held" – in other words, "mobbing" (25).

Although Kramer goes well beyond the formalism that marks much of American legal history, he adduces no direct evidence that enables him "to distinguish constitutional mob action from a simple riot" (27). Indeed, while mob action followed informal rules for how much and what kind of violence was appropriate in response to a particular abuse, most of the evidence of "the people themselves" in his book comes from elite discourse *about* popular action. True, elites like Jefferson and Madison were more likely to make reference to popular constitutionalism than opponents like Hamilton and Marshall, but Kramer is too honest an interpreter of constitutional history to assign this to evidence of social movements on behalf of popular sovereignty without direct evidence. But he only gestures toward how "the people" are engaged in any serious effort at constitutional interpretation.

2.4.3 Siegal and Her Collaborators

In over two decades as a Professor of Law at Yale, Reva Siegal and her collaborators have moved closer than either Ackerman or Kramer to the social movement canon.[16] This is in part because of her prodigious capacity to read and digest work from a number of traditions, but it also comes from her concept of "constitutional culture," which is quite close to social movement scholars' concept of framing."[17] Siegel, in her 2008–9 article on *Heller,* explicitly adopted the social movement "framing" concept, arguing that "originalism" went well beyond Supreme Court doctrine. She returned to this theme in an article penned shortly after the Supreme Court's thunderous liquidation of *Roe* in the *Dobbs* decision. In "Memory Games," Siegel (2023) wrote that originalism is not simply a value-neutral method of interpreting the Constitution, but a political practice whose long-term goal was overturning *Roe.*

Beginning at the turn of the century, Siegel gave increasing attention to the right's constitutional doctrines, and, in particular, to "originalism." In a series of articles written either on her own or with collaborators, she saw originalists' legal reasoning as not legal at all but the result of a carefully constructed social movement ideology. The Trumpian court-packing with conservative judges

---

[16] Siegel's contributions to the debate about movements include, most notably, "Text in Context: Gender and the Constitution from a Social Movement Perspective" (2000), "'She the People': The Nineteenth Amendment, Sex Equality, Federalism and the Family" (2002), "Dead or Alive: Originalism as Popular Constitutionalism" (2008–9), and most recently, "Memory Games: Dobbs's Originalism as Anti-Democratic Living Constitutionalism – and Some Pathways for Resistance" (2023). Also see Balkin and Siegel (2006), Post and Siegel (2007), and Post (2006).

[17] For the origins of the "framing perspective" in social movement theorizing, see Snow et al. (1986).

accelerated the speed of the movement from civil society to law. In her work, Siegel moved progressively in the direction of social movement theorizing. For example, in "Principles, Practices, and Social Movements," Balkin and Siegel (2006: 928–9) argue that:

> As social movements challenge the conventions that regulate the application of principles, longstanding principles can call into question the legitimacy of customary practices ... or imbue with constitutional value practices that were long judged elicit ... When movements succeed in contesting the application of constitutional principles, they can help change the social meaning of constitutional principles and the practices they regulate.

In "Memory Games," Siegel (2023) highlights the politics of judicial appointments. These matter critically to originalism's authority, as do appeals to constitutional memory to legitimate the exercise of public power. Examining these different dimensions of originalism's authority, "Memory Games" shows that the conservative legal movement has practiced originalism as a general ideological orientation rather than a constitutional doctrine. To demonstrate how this has worked, Siegel sees originalism's origin as a "backlash"[18] to the decisions of the Warren and Burger Courts. *Dobbs* showed just how far the backlash against the Warren Court went in building a countermovement with its main expressions in the courts and in the public interest groups founded by the Right.

In her work, Siegel has gestured toward the deep social and political changes that lie behind such decisions as *Dobbs,* but she has not drawn the causal lines very clearly. "For example," writes Michael McCann, "the Heritage Foundation and the Federalist Society are not responses to specific liberal/left movements, but a response to a variety of movements and issues in an effort to change the entire political, social, and economic structure of the U.S."[19] What social scientists like David Meyer and Suzanne Staggenborg (1996, 1998) call "countermovements," are often expressions of deeper structural conflicts that are disguised by the niceties of legal reasoning and litigation.

2.4.4 Klarman and Legal Backlash

In his path-breaking book *From Jim Crow to Civil Rights*, legal historian Klarman (2004) laid out a narrative of the relations among the courts, the Congress, the Civil Rights movement and the counter-movement against

---

[18] Personal communication. SeeSection 4, for our discussion of what we prefer to call "movement-countermovement interaction."

[19] The quotation is extracted from McCann's detailed and thoughtful comments on an earlier version of this Element.

them. *Brown,* to summarize Klarman's dense argument in a few words, led to the formation of a "countermovement" and to what, both in this book and in the book that followed, *From the Closet to the Altar: Courts, Backlash, and the Struggle for Same-Sex Marriage* (2013), he calls "backlash." In the latter book, Klarman (2013: x) writes:

> When the Court intervenes to defend a minority position or even to resolve an issue that divides the country down the middle, its decisions can generate political backlash, especially when the losers are intensely committed, politically organized, and geographically concentrated.

Many scholars have covered the history of the post-*Brown* backlash in the South and elsewhere against the decisions of the Warren Court. Klarman's most original contribution was *interactive* – inserting the actions of a new generation of movement activists at the heart of the story. He showed how a new phase of activism moved the Johnson Administration and its congressional allies to pass landmark laws extending civil and voting rights to minorities. That activism was the intervening mechanism between the segregationist upsurge in the South and the shift of the Democrats toward more deliberate support for Black rights.

This was the beginning of an interactive approach to law, politics, and movements in American legal history. It was also central to Klarman's *From the Closet to the Alter,* a history of the relationship among the conservative countermovement that interacted with the movement to bring about same-sex marriage (Dorf and Tarrow 2013). In both of his books, Klarman inserted movement/institutional interaction within the formalism of court-centered legal analysis. But in neither of his books did Klarman draw upon the theoretical work on movement/countermovement interaction that had developed in social movement studies (Meyer and Staggenborg 1996). Beginning in the 1990s, the distance between these two bodies of scholarship began to narrow, beginning with the debate between Gerald Rosenberg and Michael McCann on the capacity of court-made law to effect social change.

3 Crossovers and Convergences

In 1991, political scientist Gerald Rosenberg published his path-breaking book, *The Hollow Hope,* in which he carefully assessed the social and political implications of the *Brown* and other court decisions. The subtitle of his book, "Can Courts Bring About Social Change?" encapsulated the question that has preoccupied both lawyers and social scientists since then: "Not very well," was his conclusion, backed up by a mountain of statistical and other evidence.

But Rosenberg's causal arrows went in only one direction – from court decisions to their implementation to the effect of the latter on society in general and inequality in particular. Nowhere in his book was there evidence of the interactive relationships among cause lawyers, the people they represent, the movements of which both are a part, and the institutions that either lay down the law or fail to do so.

3.1 Responses to *The Hollow Hope*

Rosenberg's book ignited a firestorm of research and controversy, one that would inform scholarship on law and courts around the world. What provoked legal scholars and social scientists alike was Rosenberg's hypothesis that investing in litigation takes resources and attention away from other forms of collective action which might have had a more powerful effect on inequality than going to court. This was a one-way empirical statement that elided the complex interactions among courts, movements, and the constituencies they claimed to represent.

In his book-length study of the campaign to end gender-based inequality in wages in the United States, *Rights at Work,* McCann (1994) also offered an ontological critique of Rosenberg's book, arguing that his "model of causation was instrumental, linear, and unidirectional (McCann 2006: 459) and thus missed some of the more external consequences of legal litigation. The constructivist alternative, McCann argued, avoids the tendency toward oversimplification and over-determination and allows space for human agency as well as for multiple intersubjective social and contextual factors.

McCann's take on Rosenberg's book was part of a new trend in the social sciences toward the fusion of social science methods with legal activism. His book showed that while pay equity litigation often failed to result in positive rulings, it indirectly affected social outcomes, offering mobilizers an understanding of legal rights which then influenced how workers and management interacted. In McCann's (1994) reading, the language of the law converted what otherwise might have been wishes into rights and obligations.

In his rejoinder to McCann, Rosenberg (2006) argued that moving away from positivism inhibits our ability to "answer the most important and interesting questions," including – in the gender-inequality cases that were the focus of McCann's book – the relative impact of law, union organizing, and social protest on pay equity reform. Offering an alternate reading of McCann's evidence, he argued that *Rights at Works* showed that courts can help progressive and labor forces, but only under conditions that occur infrequently and are virtually determinative of change on their own. Contentious as it was, the Rosenberg/McCann debate signaled the beginning of a fusion between socio-legal and social movement scholarship.

While this debate has continued to develop in too many ways to adequately detail here, as new generations of scholars have taken up the core questions that motivated both Rosenberg and McCann, we want to highlight one development in particular: What Rosenberg's account also missed was that "losing" in court could lead to "winning outside of court." As NeJaime (2011: 954) observed after an exhaustive review of the literature,

> ...scholars who stress the indirect benefits of litigation credit Brown with fueling a powerful social movement by raising consciousness, driving fund-raising, legitimizing a cause, and influencing other state actors ... This approach decouples success from the implementation and enforcement of judicial orders and focuses on the discursive and political power of courts' pronouncements.

In his analysis, NeJaime went further than the early Rosenberg critics by distinguishing between the *internal* and the *external* benefits of litigation. By *internal* effects he referred to those relating to the movement itself; by *external* ones he referred to movements' relations with other actors – political parties, institutions, other movements, and ordinary citizens (NeJaime 2011: 954–5). In fact, so suspicious was he of court-based outcomes that he specified a number of positive outcomes for social change resulting from movements that lose their cases in the courts. Rather than a one-way causal direction from courts to movements to social change, NeJaime sees movements at the core of a dynamic and interactive set of relationships.

3.2 "Real-World" Influences

After the turn of the century, legal scholars began to move beyond debating Rosenberg's findings to make a broader effort to understand the broader relations between movements and the law. In an article entitled "The Social Movement Turn in Law," Cummings (2016: 1) reported that:

> ...from 1970 to 1985, there were 96 articles in Westlaw's Law Reviews and Journals database referencing "social movement" .... From 1985 to 2000, the number climbed to 1,893 ... ; since then (as of January 1, 2015), there have been 7,850 articles ... References in the past 15 years have more than quadrupled in absolute terms and doubled in percentage terms over the prior period.[20]

---

[20] Also see Cummings (2017a) and Cummings and NeJaime (2010).

The fusion between legal and movement studies was advanced by the growing evidence of inequality in western capitalist societies. In 2021, Kate Andrias and Benjamin Sachs offered a bold analysis in their "Law and Organizing in an Era of Political Inequality." In the same year, Catherine Albiston, Scott Cummings, and Richard Abel offered an examination of activist formation in their "Making Public Interest Lawyers in a Time of Crisis," and Amna Akbar, Sameer Ashar, and Joclyn Simonson (2021) offered a sweeping analysis of what they called "Movement Law."

This trend was not limited to the United States or to "The West." In the UK, Hilson (2002) and Vanhala (2012) applied social movement theory to the British and European environmental and other social movements. Scholars of Asian politics also drew on social movement insights to examine the use of law to pursue social change in China (Stern 2013; Liu and Halliday 2016; Gallagher 2017), Hong Kong (Tam 2013), Japan, Korea (Arrington 2019a, 2019b), Myanmar (Chua 2018) and Singapore (Chua 2014).[21] The same goes for those working on other regions as well (see, e.g., Wilson and Rodriguez Cordero 2006; Wilson 2009; Gallagher 2017, 2022; Wilson and Gianella-Malca 2019; and Taylor 2020, 2023b, among others on Latin America).

The evidence of growing inequality led a number of scholars to revive the study of the labor movement as a *movement.* In *Blue and Green,* Cummings (2018a) examined the drive for social justice in the Port of Los Angeles. In the same year, in an article about the strategic mobilization of human rights framing against blacklisting in the United Kingdom, Kahraman (2018) predicted "A New Era for Labor Activism." More recently, McCann, writing with George Lovell (2020), returned to the interactions between law and labor in their *Union by Law: Filipino American Labor Activists, Rights Radicalism, and Racial Capitalism.* The result is that the relations between labor as a movement and the law have become one of the leading edges in the fusion of social movement and legal scholarship.[22]

At about the same time, European integration stimulated notable steps toward the study of transnational legal mobilization. In a flurry of works after the turn of the century, Karen Alter and Jeanette Vargas (2000), Conant (2002), Rhonda Evans Case and Terri Givens (2010), and Daniel Keleman (2011) drew scholarly attention to the intersection of law and movements. The same can be said for the development of international and

---

[21] See also Lynette Chua, David Engel, and Sida Liu's *The Asian Law and Society Reader* (2023).

[22] A major effort to bring together these topics with the study of forms of repression of labor is Fisk and Reddy (2020).

regional courts both inside (Cichowski 2007; Alter 2014) and outside (Sikkink 2011) of Europe.[23]

3.3 Advancing toward Fusion

In the rest of this section, we will briefly summarize five areas of scholarship in which we see important advances in the convergence of legal and social movement studies. We hope to highlight

- *First*, scholars who have worked to map the conditions that shape the ability of movements to bring legal claims before the courts.
- *Second*, progress in assessing the ability of movements to alter the law itself, create new law and/or alter judicial interpretations of existing law.
- *Third*, growing efforts to track the ability of movements to shape debates about legal issues, both among those who might identify as members of those movements, as well as among the broader public.
- *Fourth,* analyses of how the courts – and the law more generally – shape movement strategies and outcomes.
- *Fifth,* the turn to comparative studies of law and social movements and efforts to examine the growing relationship domestic and international venues for activism.

3.3.1 Claim-Making in the Courts

Increasingly, scholars working in the socio-legal tradition have taken on some of the early critiques of the use of law by social movements. For one thing, they argued that the turn to legal claim-making does not necessarily reflect a belief in the efficacy or legitimacy of the law – in fact these efforts may be strategic (McCann 1994; Ewick and Silbey 1998; Lovell 2012) or even driven by ambivalence (Taylor 2018).

They also complicate the notions that legal strategies are unduly expensive. The cost of litigation for movement organizations varies substantially across contexts and types of litigation strategies. As Vanhala (2011: 23) notes:

> [T]he assumption that litigation will always be the most expensive route to successfully influencing policy has not been demonstrably confirmed across a wide range of policy fields. Different types of litigation strategies, each with varying resource thresholds, can be employed ... [I]f the organization is acting as the litigant, this is undoubtedly an expensive strategy; submitting third-party participant briefs to influence the court's reasoning is generally less costly and time consuming.[24]

---

[23] We thank Celeste Arrington for this insight.

[24] Vanhala points to the fact that, in some contexts, litigation is relatively inexpensive. Countries throughout Latin America, for example, have developed legal procedures that, at least in theory,

Others challenged Rosenberg's conclusion that the turn to law necessarily demobilizes would-be supporters and provokes backlash. As McCann (1994) demonstrated, unsuccessful litigation on wage discrimination in California, Connecticut, and Washington did not spur the end of mobilization; instead, it prompted the growth of the movement. Later scholars argued that the relative mobilization and backlash possibilities of litigation are mixed. For example, in her study of compensation litigation in East Asia, Arrington (2019b) identified five interacting mechanisms – attribution of similarity, brokerage, issue dramatization, political cover, and intergroup discussions – that help to explain the indirect positive *and* negative effects of litigation.

Subsequent studies focusing on various causes in different parts of the world show that litigation can draw new members into movements and help to head off or mitigate backlash. For instance, Kahraman (2018: 1302) documented how blacklisted construction workers in the United Kingdom were able to pursue a litigation-based strategy at the European Court of Human Rights, while simultaneously "establish[ing] new networks, strengthen[ing] existing ties with legal professionals, academics, and other pro-labor organizations, leverag-[ing] media attention, and forg[ing] a new collective identity." Litigation – to return to an earlier theme in this article – did not preclude these other possibilities.

Further, when it comes to backlash, Keck (2009: 182) reminds us that the most pressing question is "compared to what?" As he notes, "all political strategies employed by or on behalf of the relatively disadvantaged are likely to be met with powerful political resistance, and all such strategies are unlikely to help those most desperately in need." Mobilization efforts outside the law are also met with backlash, countermovements, and counter-mobilization (Meyer and Staggenborg 1996). Whether social movement engagement with law provokes more or less backlash than other strategies is highly context specific.

3.3.2 Making New Law and Introducing New Interpretations

Increasingly, scholars have taken an interest in how social movements attempt to alter the ways in which laws are drafted and interpreted. Movement organizations both seek to educate judges about specific kinds of problems and convince them of new ways of understanding legal issues. Hollis-Brusky (2015), for example, shows that the conservative legal movement was able to push a particular ideological view within the US judiciary by engaging in repeated "pedagogical" interventions and advocating for the nomination of

---

allow individuals to initiate cases without need of a lawyer and without docket fees (Brewer-Carías 2009).

conservative judges, rather than by prioritizing litigation for conservative causes.[25] Movement organizations also participate as parties to litigation with the primary goal of trying to reshape judges' understandings of the issues.

Ezequiel González-Ocantos (2014, 2016) likewise demonstrates how activists in Latin America were able to introduce and support new arguments about human rights protections to sympathetic and indifferent judges. Where judges were opposed to human rights and transitional justice discourse, the activists pushed instead for personnel changes within the judiciary. Social movements or, more precisely, the NGOs or lawyers associated with them, often file amicus curiae briefs that offer legal interpretations related to particular cases. Pavone (2022) reveals a similar dynamic at work in the use of European law within the domestic courts of European Union countries.[26]

Cichowski (2007) documents that this practice is not limited to domestic courts. She shows that amicus filings have been particularly influential at the European Court of Human Rights. These amicus briefs can shift the ways judges think about issues or cases, ultimately resulting in changes in judicial decision-making. Because, as Cichowski (2007: 11) writes, "judicial rulings can also have a more indirect impact on movement activity by changing the rules and procedures in a way that makes the policy process more open to a particular group," there are radiating effects of these pedagogical interventions. Ximena Soley (2019) finds that movement organizations play a similar role in Inter-American system.

In other work, one of us explores how public exposure to problems, "where an issue becomes visible to judges in their lived experience outside the courtroom as well as legible to judges as legal in nature," can also increase judicial receptivity (Taylor 2023b: 51–2). Here, the intervention of social movements or other societal actors does not come through pedagogical interventions related to specific legal arguments. Instead, the quantity of legal claims is key:

> [T]he persistence and/or increase of claims related to a specific grievance cumulatively inform judges about an issue, making them comfortable with the scope of the issue, making them more aware of the issue's salience, and making then identify with claimants. This can spark a consideration or reconsideration about the correct legal response to that issue – and therefore those claims. (52)

As is often the case with pedagogical interventions, however, the influx of cases can instead backfire, prompting judges to hold fast to old views on the issue

---

[25] See also Teles (2010).

[26] For Pavone, part of the explanation for the success of these interventions is the workload facing judges. At least some of the time, they happily offload the work of deciding cases to lawyers willing to "ghostwrite" decisions.

(Kim et al. 2021). Yet, when judges view the cases or issues in question as violating locally specific understandings of dignity or other socio-legal values, these interventions can change judges' minds (Taylor 2023b).

3.3.3 Shaping Legal Debates and Interpretations

Social movement scholars have also shown how often movements become involved in contests over meaning, hoping to socialize or persuade target audiences – whether the general public or specific state officials – of a particular interpretation of reality. In doing so, they have drawn on the social movement tradition of "framing" analysis from the work of David Snow et al. (1986). As McCann (1994) examined in his *Rights at Work,* contestation over meaning can be particularly important with respect to law and rights. Even when litigation is stymied within the courts, efforts at legal mobilization may have "downstream" consequences, encouraging individuals to join movements and constraining employers (and other powerful actors) in the future. In *Union by Law*, McCann and George Lovell (2020: 308) found that a rule by the Equal Employment Opportunities Commission (EEOC) amended its interpretation of the Federal Rules of Civil Procedure to enable claimants of unfair employment practices "to band together against a common adversary" under a theory of "diverse impact."

Along these lines, argues Leslie Thiele (1993: 282), "[t]he importance of social movements is often observable *in the creation of a background of social and political understandings and orientations* that are participated in (for various reasons) by state officials, business leaders, and the general public" (italics added). Despite the formal orientation of the judicial branch – its independence, its insulation from both the public, from other branches of government, and, at least in democratic theory, from the parties to disputes – this is perhaps especially true in the realm of law. US Supreme Court deliberations on cases with major social implications are now often accompanied by courthouse protests and other mass demonstrations. The causal impact of general public opinion trends on Supreme Court decisions has become the subject of vigorous debate (Johnson and Strother 2021), as is the impact of the preferences of specific audiences for judicial decision-making (Baum 2008).

Social movements also seek to shape public discourse about particular court cases or legal issues, persuading or otherwise socializing state and non-state actors to view issues in a particular way. Movements or networks of activists "contribute to changing perceptions that both state and societal actors may have of their identities, interests, and preferences, to transforming their discursive positions, and ultimately to changing procedures, policies, and behaviors"

(Keck and Sikkink 1998: 3). As Claudia Junghjyun Kim and Celeste Arrington (2023) show in their investigation of mobilization against US military bases in East Asian countries, "movements use court-recognized standing, legal framing, judges' examination of evidence, the rhythm of court proceedings, and rulings to gain authority, bring information to light, and thereby reshape public knowledge."

3.3.4 How Courts Impact Movements

While movements impact judges, courts, and the law itself, an increasing trend in the new scholarship on law and movements shows that the inverse can also be true. Movements are shaped by laws on the books, by access to the courts, and by judicial proclivities. Legal institutions and actors form part of the "opportunity structure" for movements, shaping the strategic and tactical choices available to them (Hilson 2010; Prabhat 2016; de Fazio 2012; Boutcher 2013; Boutcher and Stobaugh 2013). For example, rules on standing will limit the kinds of claims and claimants that can come before judges, and judicial receptivity will influence decisions and remedies offered (Vanhala 2011). Courts can in some cases encourage changes in venue – for example, from state to federal courts or vice versa – and subnational differences in judicial receptivity – for example, across court districts or even judges within districts – can influence the kinds of claims that activists are likely to file or the timing of their claims.

Actors opposed to particular movements or causes can also try to use the formal legal system, when opportunity structures allow, to limit the ability of movements to protest or otherwise engage in contentious politics. For example, corporations can put forward what are called "strategic lawsuits against public participation" or SLAPPs (Canan and Pring 1988; Vanhala 2022). These suits typically involve defamation, torts, conspiracy, constitutional civil rights violations, or nuisance claims (Pring 1989). However, in such cases, the goal of the plaintiff is less to win the case (often, the facts simply are not there) and more to intimidate or burden the defendants, leading them to cease any movement-related activity. Some of the time, these efforts backfire, empowering movements, as they file counter-claims and seek to win framing battles in the media (Hilson 2016).

New laws and new court decisions can also legitimate a cause, offering official state recognition to that cause and inviting new members to associate with movements, in the process expanding movements (Faux 1988; Staggenborg 1991; McCann 1994; Balkin 2011). In this way, rights and law can be a common reference point for otherwise disconnected actors that allows for the creation of a collective identity and a mobilizing coalition (Adam 2017).

At the same time, many scholars have cautioned against a reliance on law, courts, and "rights talk" (Glendon 1991; Nonet and Selznick 2001; Alviar García et al. 2016). An emphasis on rights and legal frames can give primacy to individualized, rather than collective claims (Marshall 2003), though the filing of these individual claims may eventually lead to collective action (Albiston 2005). The language and procedures of courts may also have a moderating impact on movements, and Julieta Lemaitre and Rachel Sieder (2017) show in their in-depth case study of mobilization by both feminists and religious conservatives around Inter-American Court of Human Rights cases. Further, legal wins can prompt backlash from voters and politicians, ultimately undermining the cause in question (Rosenberg 1991; Klarman 2004, 2013). These backlash or movement-countermovement dynamics, however, will not always cut cleanly in one direction or another (Keck 2009). This is why – in the following section – we will place great emphasis on the political or legal opportunity structure within which movement actors make their moves.

3.3.5 Taking the Comparative Cure

In recent decades, a growing number of scholars have adopted a comparative approach to law and movements in attempting to understand the gap between law as it is written and law as it is experienced or understood by different social groups. A good deal of this work has compared similar liberal systems – mainly in North America and Europe – but it has increasingly ranged beyond these areas to countries in which new or revised constitutions have been installed and in which there has been what some scholars have called "the judicialization of politics."[27] Much of this work – and thus much of this section – track contexts defined by liberal legalism, though scholars have increasingly found creative ways to study law in authoritarian contexts (see Hendley 1999; Trochev 2008; Tezcür 2009; Tam 2013; Chua 2014, 2019; Moustafa 2014; Gallagher 2017; among others) as well as the ways that illiberalism plays out in ostensibly liberal contexts (McCann and Kahraman 2021). We cannot hope to fully cover this ever-growing body of scholarship, but we trace several of the major throughlines in this section.

In *The Rights Revolution,* Epp (1998) drew on the social movement theory of "resource mobilization" (McCarthy and Zald 1977). Epp built his book around the concept of "support structures" for litigation. A support structure consists of "rights-advocacy organizations, supportive lawyers, and sources of financing" (23) which can serve to balance the unequal power relations between actors

---

[27] For a review of this literature, see Botero et al. (2022).

seeking change and those favoring the status quo. Social movement organizations may have a particular impact as components of a support structure for litigation (Cichowski 2007; Vanhala 2010). Others, like Ezequiel González-Ocantos (2016), implicitly drew on resource mobilization theory too. He showed that human rights activists in Latin America were able to introduce and support new arguments about rights protections to sympathetic and indifferent judges through professionalization.

In a second major work, *Making Rights Real* (2009), Epp compared the impact of legal and administrative activism on three policy areas within the United States – police reform, sexual harassment reform, and the renovation of playgrounds – and through a paired comparison of police reform in the United States and the United Kingdom. The combination of intra-system with inter-system comparison was a novel innovation, facilitated by the fact that Britain and the United States share similar systems of common law. The comparison of movement activism in similar legal systems was also carried out by Gianluca de Fazio, who cleverly compared the American civil rights movement with Northern Ireland's almost-contemporary movement for minority rights. In his work, de Fazio (2012) drew on the growing interest in legal opportunity structure among scholars in both Europe and the United States.

The concept of political opportunity structure was adopted and specified by a number of scholars working in Europe. Social movement scholars had understood political opportunity as "consistent – but not necessarily formal or permanent – dimensions of the political environment or of change in that environment that provide incentives for collective action by affecting expectations for success or failure" (Tarrow 1994: 85; Gamson and Meyer 1996). In these political opportunity analyses, however, they did not assess features of the legal system. Hilson (2002), drawing on the political process approach to social movements, put forward the term "legal opportunity" in his effort to understand how four European movements – the women's movement, the environmental movement, the lesbian and gay movement, and the animal welfare movement – navigated between tactics, including both protest and litigation. Vanhala (2010, 2011, 2012, 2018, 2022) further specified the contours of legal opportunity first in a series of studies on disability rights movements and later on climate activists. And scholars working on different Asian countries have advanced new understandings of the role of cause lawyers in social movements (Tam 2013; Liu and Halliday 2016; Arrington 2019a), as well as the complicated relationships between rights, litigation, and social change (Stern 2013; Chua 2014, 2018; Gallagher 2017).

3.3.6 From National to Transnational Law and Movements

Since much of this development has turned on the international human rights movement, this has led to an effort to explore the intersection between international and domestic lawmaking. Many of the scholars who did so explicitly applied social movement theories to their comparative work, while others have gestured toward social movements among the actors that have advanced the domestication of international laws and provisions.

EU law was the starting venue for Vanhala's work on the transfer of legal instruments from the international to the domestic level. In her work on the Aarhus Convention, Vanhala (2018) showed how the EU's efforts to advance environmental policies in the newly democratizing states of East-Central Europe were adapted by British environmental lawyers to British environmental practice. This was similar to the process by which local actors served to translate international human rights conventions, as documented by Sally Merry (2006b) in her landmark book on *Human Rights and Gender Violence* in the Global South and her 2006 article "Transnational Human Rights and Local Activism: Mapping the Middle."

The processes of "judicialization" and "vernacularization" have been central to the work of several scholars in Latin America (c.f. Sieder et al. 2005; Couso et al. 2010). Focusing on the growing tendency of countries in the Global South to include social rights in their constitutions, Daniel Brinks, Varun Gauri, and Kyle Shen (2015) argued that what they called "social rights constitutionalism" brought "human rights—or a subset of them – into domestic constitutions." Social rights constitutionalism took various forms as it was "vernacularized" from international legal venues, but it had in common that – once adopted – it induced "social actors to pursue their goals, and the increasing judicialization of political disputes under the social rights rubric" (290).[28]

In this strand of work, however, movements still tend to appear offstage.[29] This ellipsis is odd, especially given the fact that Latin America has been the site of some of the most innovative episodes of social movement politics during the same period, and that those movements often sought justice through the courts (e.g., Keck and Sikkink 1998; Sikkink 2011). Perhaps the fact that many Latin American countries were adopting different forms of social constitutionalism has been an indirect effect of their differing patterns of social movement politics (Van Cott 2000).

---

[28] Taylor (2023b) investigates a similar process, which she describes as constitutional embedding, looking at how constitutional law takes on specific meanings in social and legal life.

[29] A new chapter by Ruibal (2023) in the *Oxford Handbook of Latin American Social Movements* is a rare and notable exception.

The research efforts sketched in this section were productive initial steps toward remedying the limited cross-pollination between the fields of law and social movements and the oft-criticized "methodological nationalism" of US-based scholars.[30] In the next section, we will put forward our own synthesis, relying both on our own research and of that of other scholars to attempt to show how legal mobilization is both constrained by, and employs political and legal opportunity structures and leads routinely to what we call "movement-countermovement interaction."

4 Theorizing Law and Movements through Four Mechanisms

Section 3 showed that there have been increasing efforts to fuse social movement and legal scholarship since the late 1990s and early 2000s. An important part of this move has been the effort to substitute a more interdependent approach to the relations among courts, movements, and constituencies for the one-way causal direction we saw in the work of Rosenberg and others. In the rest of Section 4, we will build on this effort four interrelated headings: the concept of legal mobilization; the process of social construction; the employment of the legal and political opportunity structure; and the process of movement/ countermovement interaction both in and outside of the courts. In Section 5, we will illustrate our framework in two very different intersections of law and movements.

4.1 Legal Mobilization

"The legal mobilization approach," writes Douglas NeJaime, "resists the impulse to single out courts … Rather than treat the judicial ruling as the primary object of analysis, legal mobilization scholars' interpretive approach sees law as constituting social meaning in complex and dynamic ways" (NeJaime 2011: 961). But this conclusion raises a new question: so broad has the specification of "the legal" become that scholars have debated how to bound the concept of legal mobilization, disagreeing on which activities constitute the process, on the kinds of actors it targets, and on the sort of claims that fall within its range (Lehoucq and Taylor 2019). Lehoucq and Taylor (2019: 3) define legal mobilization as "the use of law in an explicit, self-conscious way through the invocation of a formal institutional mechanism," which differentiates legal mobilization from related concepts like "legal framing"[31] and "legal

---

[30] A forthcoming *Research Handbook on Law, Movements, and Social Change*, edited by Steven Boutcher, Corey Shdaimah, and Michael W. Yarbrough, currently in production, will bring many countries from the Global South into the comparative study of law and movements.

[31] As Lehoucq and Taylor (2020: 19) note, "Legal framing refers to the inclusion of legal rules, ideas, or symbols in collective action frames." Benford and Snow (2000: 614) define "collective

consciousness,"[32] while offering flexibility to scholars as they consider the use of law in bureaucratic or administrative forums, quasi-judicial procedures, and litigation.

In the legal literature, Frances Zemans was the first to explicitly advocate that "legal mobilization" should be considered as a form of political participation, rather than as something that happens outside the realm of politics. As she wrote in a path-making article in 1983; "The bulk of [legal system] activity takes place within the state and so become state actors themselves" (692). She furthered this argument by appealing to the democratic consequences of legal system engagement:

> ...the legal system can be quintessentially democratic, although not neces-
> sarily egalitarian if the competence and the means to make use of this access
> to governmental authority is not equally distributed ... [T]he share of the
> output of the political system that individuals receive is in part determined by
> the extent to which they mobilize the law on their own behalf. (693)

Not long after, social movement scholars began to engage with the legal mobilization framework. For instance, Burstein (1991) argued that when added to a social movement's repertoire of contention, it can allow movement activists to strategically diversify their tactics and targets and even engage in what Hannah Murphy and Aynsley Kellow (2013) call "forum-shopping." Legal mobilization can also influence whether claimants see themselves either as "rights-bearers" or as "victims." In the latter case, this identity may lead to despondency and a perceived loss of agency, while in the former one, this self-identification has a mobilizing effect, generating a sense of entitlement and solidarity across similarity situated individuals and to efforts at group mobilization.[33]

Some scholars have raised the concern that legal mobilization signals an acceptance of hegemonic legality propagated by the state (Glendon 1991). At the same time, empirical research has shown that, at least in certain contexts, individuals and movements use rights talk and legal tools strategically in pursuit of their goals, without necessarily buying into these underlying narratives (McCann 1994; Epp 2009; Lovell 2012). Further, legal mobilization can *undermine* these state-led narratives, as citizens directly experience the ways in which the formal legal system is not, in fact, either fair or effective (Gallagher 2006).

---

action frames" in the context of social movement scholarship as "action-oriented sets of beliefs and meanings that inspire and legitimate the activities and campaigns of a social movement organization."

[32] Merry (1990: 5) defines legal consciousness as "the ways people understand and use the law ... the way people conceive of the 'natural' and normal way of doing things, their habitual patterns of talk and action, and their common-sense understanding of the world."

[33] Others find that victim identification can, in fact, be mobilizing, suggesting that the consequences of these kinds of identities are context-specific.

In our work, we have emphasized the connection between claims advanced in the formal legal sphere and their consequences for legal consciousness in civil society. For example, in her investigation of the use of the *tutela* procedure in Colombia, Taylor (2018: 341) writes:

> When citizens make claims on the state, they are implicitly calling for changes in relationship between state and society, in the provision of goods by the state, and in the protection of rights. While the claim in question may be purely personal in nature for the individual claimant, the consequences of that claim—or the aggregation of many individual claims—are political.

Elsewhere, Taylor (2020: 1350) notes that "constitutional rights offer equal access to all citizens on paper, yet real access is determined by the ability of citizens to make claims to these goods, either as individuals or as part of a group." In this sense, legal mobilization is a core component of social and political incorporation, as rights claims in the formal legal sphere can, under certain conditions, push forward social policy change. However, this route to social and political incorporation is "one that might reify rather than offer redress for preexisting disadvantage" (1350), since access to the formal legal system is not evenly distributed, as Galanter (1974) noted in his seminal "Why the 'Haves' Come Out Ahead."

The process of legal mobilization contains both positive and negative implications, as NeJaime (2011, 2012) and Cummings (2024) clearly demonstrate. For one thing, when it succeeds, legal mobilization can "be too successful for its own good, especially when tactical disagreement arises" (NeJaime 2012: 701). And as Rosenberg argued in 1991, the successful use of the courts can crowd out other strategies both for the litigating movement and for others who follow its example. Legal mobilization can also provoke countermobilization – both in and outside the courts. At the extreme, it "can create a systemic risk of backsliding, contributing to the mobilization of law against the rule of law itself" – a phenomenon that Cummings, in his analysis of the actions of the Trump lawyers who tried to reverse the results of the 2020 US election, has labelled "anti-legal mobilization" (Cummings 2024: 5, 12–13).

4.2 The Process of Social Construction

An important development in the study of legal mobilization came from what is alternately described as a turn to constitutive (McCann 1994), social constructivist (Taylor 2020), or sociological institutionalist (Vanahla 2018) modes of analysis. These approaches were all influenced – whether explicitly or implicitly – by many of the critical legal theorists cited above, who noted that legal practices and discourses are meaning-making.[34] As McCann and Lovell put it in their recent book *Union by Law* (2020: 357):

> In this constructivist approach, formal pronouncements by authoritative decision makers such as judges matter as much through their indirect, "radiating" effects on individuals' routine identities, perceptions of legitimate entitlement, actionable risks, opportunities, possibilities, and strategic resources as through enforceable commands.

McCann and Lovell illuminate core features of the process of legal mobilization, including the social construction of the grievances that form the basis of legal claims and the process of acquiring the legal knowledge that allows for claim-making. They were not alone: As Charles Epp noted in his 1998 book, cases do not come before the courts "as if by magic." Instead, there is a process by which individuals or groups come to view something in their lives as a problem that can or should be resolved through the legal system.

Social movement scholars have long considered the importance of "collective action frames," which refer to "action-oriented sets of beliefs and meanings that inspire and legitimate the activities and campaigns of a social movement organization" (Benford and Snow 2000: 61). In parallel, even if they do not always explicitly refer to the law as a "frame," socio-legal scholars consider how law serves to constitute everyday social interactions. Legal mobilization works to shape social understandings of particular issues as legal in nature, a process that Taylor (2020) describes as "the social construction of legal grievances."

Paris (2009) was one of the first to transfer the concept of framing from the social movement canon to the legal field. NeJaime soon after argued that how courts framed the issue of same-sex marriage had a profound impact on the LGBTQ movement (NeJaime 2012). But social *re*construction was also the result of how the LGBTQ movement framed the issue to appeal to voters. As Nan Hunter (2017: 1662) wrote, they "set out to change social and constitutional meanings not primarily through courts or legislatures, but with a strategy designed to win over moveable middle voters in ballot question elections

The recognition of social construction in the social movement field goes back to Francesca Polletta's investigation of the work of civil rights organizers in the US South in the 1960s. Polletta (2000: 369) found that rights talk allowed for the reframing and re-envisioning of conditions on the ground. More recently, in her work on the *tutela* in Colombia, Taylor (2020: 1331) showed how "societal actors encourage potential claimants to view a specific problem through the lens of the law and to make claims in the formal legal system rather than doing

---

[34] See especially Haney-López (1997) on this point.

nothing or advancing a claim in some other setting." At the same time, repeated exposure to new legal claims encourages judges to rethink the way they understood the law and accept these news claims, expanding rights protections in the process.

An early recognition of the power of social construction was Eskridge's (2001) observation that the power of the *Brown* decision went well beyond the issue of school segregation; it would serve as a lesson for the Montgomery bus boycott soon after. But having constructed something as a legal grievance is not enough to ensure that legal mobilization actually occurs. Legal knowledge is part of that equation as well. As Mary Gallagher has shown in her single- (2006, 2017) and co-authored works (Gallagher and Yang 2017), the spread of information through the media or by word of mouth, as well as individual efforts at self-education can take the place of formal education in helping potential claimants overcome barriers to advancing claims in the legal system.

When individuals or groups come to see certain issues as legal grievances and have knowledge about the way the law ought to work, the experience of filing legal claims can have diverse effects. Some of the time, what Gallagher (2006: 785–6) calls "informed disenchantment" may occur. If despondency sets in, such understandings can inhibit the turn to legal mobilization in the future among both experienced and would-be claimants.

Movement actors can also reinterpret the meaning of law and rights in light of religious beliefs, customs, and other normative orders, in the process affecting how legal experts and other officials think about and understand the law. Ezequiel González-Ocantos (2014, 2016), whose work we highlighted above, shows how activists can draw on international norms to shift domestic understandings. Similarly, in an investigation of legal pluralism in India, Randeria (2007: 42) holds that:

> Social movements and NGOs in India assume salience as mediators of national and international laws at the local level but also as channels for the assertion of customary law and traditional collective rights of communities in the national arena and in international fora. NGOs linked to grassroots movements are equally important in mobilizing dissenting knowledge in order to formulate alternative people's laws and policies by using a variety of norms from different sources.

And as David Engel and Jaruwan Engel (2010) demonstrate in their study of legal consciousness in Thailand, religious beliefs and local customs may also influence the social construction of understandings about law and rights, impacting when people chose whether or not to make legal claims and how to otherwise mobilize or resolve their problems.

Thus, social movements and other social actors are involved in the social construction of rights and law, as well as the social construction of other phenomena in relation to right and the law. This brings us to the used of legal and political opportunity structures on legal mobilization.

4.3 Employing the Legal-Political Opportunity Structure

"In recent years," wrote Ellen Ann Andersen in 2005, "the concept of political opportunity structure has emerged as the most promising method of integrating the emergence, progress, and outcomes of social movements with the social context in which they operate" (48). Within the "political process model" from which the concept emerged, scholars defined it to refer to "consistent – but not necessarily formal or permanent – dimensions of the political environment that provide incentives for people to undertake collective action by affecting their expectations for success or failure" (Tarrow 2022: 143). But this overly structuralist conception of opportunities was static; Jack Goldstone and Charles Tilly (2001: 182) redefined the concept as "any changes that shift [perceived] possibility that social protest actions will lead to success in achieving a desired outcome."

The converse of opportunity is "threat," which "relates to the risks and costs of action or inaction rather than to the prospect of success" (Goldstone and Tilly 2001: 183). For example, in 2022, the British government pushed through a tough new "public order" bill designed to stop protesters from obstructing transport networks, interfering with national infrastructure and engaging in "locking-in" tactics by gluing themselves to roads, vehicles, or buildings. But threats can also trigger mobilization when they are perceived as unjust or unfairly targeted on particular groups. It is the changing opportunity and threat that triggers the mobilization of insurgent actors.

Political opportunities expand through mechanisms in the environment like *increasing access, shifting alignments, divisions among elites, and the presence of influential allies*. These mechanisms often operate in combination. For example, splits among elites, and political realignments often work together to induce disaffected groups to seek support from outsiders. This is what happened in the 1940s and 1950s, when the NAACP launched the sustained legal campaign that culminated in the *Brown* case, which began when Thurgood Marshall and others perceived a significant shift in Federal civil rights cases.

Although opportunities are influenced by the institutional structure – for example, by federalism, which offers activists opportunities for venue- or forum-shopping (Meyer and Staggenborg 1998; Szymanski 2003) – opportunities can also change contingently (Tarrow 1996). As a notable example of contingency, the Great Migration to the North enabled African Americans to use their newly won electoral power to exercise political influence in states like New York which were electorally divided and were thus responsive to the new factor of a black bloc vote.[35]

In her book on the gay rights movement in the United States, Andersen (2005: 7) drew directly on political opportunity theory to enumerate three sub-mechanisms that influenced the ability of movements to pursue law-based goals: "*access to the formal institutional structure, availability of allies*, and the *configuration of power with respect to relevant issues/challengers.*" To these, she added a fourth – "the *underlying political culture,* or, less inclusively, the alignment of the cognitive frames that mediate between opportunity and action: "So, for example, the feminist claim of a woman's right to her own body makes sense only in a cultural context that embodies notions of individual autonomy and citizen equality" (8).

Like the broader concept of political opportunity, legal opportunity encompasses both structural and contingent factors. Vanhala (2018: 112) notes that "at least three factors matter across jurisdictions and across policy areas: legal stock, standing rules, and rules on costs." These vary across nations, over time, and even – in some ways – between the legal systems of different subnational units.

Theories of legal opportunity rest implicitly on assumptions about the beliefs of the actors involved. Opportunities must be understood as such to be acted on – which connects opportunities to framing. As McAdam wrote in his seminal study of the "black insurgency" in the United States, "Mediating between opportunity and action are people and the subjective meanings they attach to their situation" (McAdam 1982: 48). Accessing legal opportunity is thus subjective, flexible, and contingent.

An important reason for aligning the larger concept of political opportunities with the more specific one of legal opportunities is that social movements often employ strategies that bridge courts, representative institutions, and protest. Hilson (2002: 239), who carried out the earliest explorations of legal opportunity structure in the United Kingdom, placed "all three strategies – lobbying, litigation, and protest – within a coherent analytical framework." Of course, even if it is chosen for contingent reasons, a given strategy may become engrained in a movement's repertoire, as employing the courts did for the NAACP in the 1950s and 1960s.[36] In the debate over *Brown*, cognate issues

---

[35] We are grateful to Michael Klarman for reminding us of this contingent opportunity in one of the author's home states.

[36] Coglianese (2001) provides a useful analysis of the institutionalization of the environmental movement in the United States. That this was not an inevitable trend has been demonstrated with

that agitated the budding civil rights movement – like job discrimination, segregation on public transport, unequal zoning and housing, and access to credit – came to play an important role in mobilizing the African-American community and its allies but were not easily transferred to the courtroom.

Actors can often create new opportunities for themselves and for others who take advantage of the paths they have opened up (Vanhala 2018; Arrington 2019a; Gallagher 2022; Tarrow 2022: 150–2). On occasion, these openings create new opportunities, as Taylor (2023b) found in research on the embedding of social constitutionalism in Colombia. When that country passed a new constitution in 1991, there was little evidence that the tutela procedure, which enabled citizens to go to a court on behalf of their "fundamental" constitutional rights, would lead to a massive opening of opportunities for both ordinary citizens and movement groups to use the court system on behalf of social rights. But its ease of access for ordinary citizens and its repeated use hardened the new opportunity into a structure of opportunities.

While open political systems offer both structural and contingent opportunities, challengers in authoritarian systems (Bunce and Wolchik 2011), or in violent democratic ones (Lemaitre and Sandvik 2017) have to rely on contingent opportunities. For example, when, in 1989, the government of the German Democratic Republic (GDR) collapsed, ordinary citizens across the Soviet Bloc took advantage of this contingent opportunity to overthrow their Communist governments.

4.4 Movement-Countermovement Interaction

In Section 3, we showed how effectively Michael Klarman used the concept of backlash. But backlash against the *Brown* decision was a one-way effect. Mobilization that impinges on the interests or values of other actors frequently stimulates those actors to respond, often setting up a movement-countermovement interaction that can become a permanent routine both in the courts or in the broader political system. Although countermovements have been familiar to social scientists since the 1980s, the term was mainly employed only to describe movements of the right that responded to the then-advancing movements of the left (Mottl 1980). Countermovements can also involve progressive actors mobilizing in reaction to Far Right movements (Vüllers and Hellmeier 2022).

In the 1990s, social movement scholars began to use the term "countermovement" to describe any movement that arises in response to a pre-existing or simultaneous one. Meyer and Staggenborg defined a countermovement as "a

---

the upsurge of disruptive protest in Europe and elsewhere on the part of a new, youth-based radical ecological movement.

movement that makes contrary claims simultaneously to those of the original movement" (1631). In a subsequent piece, these authors applied their theory to movement-countermovement interaction in two federal systems – Canada and the United States – showing how institutions intervened in the relations between movements and countermovements (1998: 210).

Meyer and Staggenborg (2022) enumerated three main facets of movements, later expanded to five, that are likely to trigger countermovements. First, when a movement shows signs of success, opponents are likely to want to emulate it, trying out similar strategies to pursue different goals. Second, when the movement threatens established interests, they are likely to want to strike back. Third, the availability of political allies encourages the formation of a countermovement. Fourth, social media and internet communications allow for the rapid diffusion of movement ideas and their countering by a countermovement. Fifth, resources facilitate countermovement mobilization.

Countermovements often avail themselves of the same opportunities as the movements they challenge, while engaging in framing battles around the nature of grievances. This was the case for the pro-and-anti abortion movements, both of which turned to the courts to advance their claims, as well as the LGBT rights movement and anti-movements (Dugan 2004). But countermovements often turn to other venues for their challenges, as the segregationist movement did in the South after the *Brown* decision when it used both state legislatures and subversive violence to attack the anti-segregationist African American movement in the South (Klarman 2013).

One of the longest-lasting movement/countermovement interaction in American history has been over the issue of abortion. Staggenborg showed in her earlier work (1991) that as the pro-choice movement began to form in the 1960s, "right to life" groups began to form at the state level and a National Right to Life Committee formed in 1971. The turning point came in 1973, when the Supreme Court decided the landmark case of *Roe* v. *Wade*,[37] which forced recalcitrant states to legalize a woman's right to choose, sparking a national countermovement against abortion. Meyer and Staggenborg (2022: 34) found that, "[b]locked by the courts, countermovement activists turned to Congress, where they lobbied unsuccessfully for a "Human Life Amendment" before getting Congress to pass the Hyde Amendment banning federal funding of abortion in 1976."

In the meantime, the courts were not sitting still: In the case of *Webster* v. *Reproductive Health Services*,[38] the Supreme Court permitted states to pass restrictions on abortion, which encouraged the anti-abortion movement to work

---

[37] 410 U.S. 113 (1973).   [38] 492 U.S. 833 (1989).

for state laws that might generate a case that could overturn *Roe.* "The pattern continued with the 1992 Supreme Court decision in *Planned Parenthood of Southeastern Pennsylvania* v. *Casey,*[39] which allowed some key restrictions on abortion but did not overturn *Roe. Casey* triggered a new – and longer – round of both judicial and political conflict over abortion.

The question of a woman's right to choose became so central to American politics that Supreme Court nominations began to turn on candidates' positions on abortion. Gradually, but with increasing militancy, anti-abortion forces built a majority on the Supreme Court, resulting in its breathtaking reversal of Roe in the landmark decision in *Dobbs* v. *Jackson Women's Health*[40] in 2022. *Dobbs'* reversal of *Roe* and *Casey* not only demonstrated a classical movement-countermovement interaction, but also showed that such interactions cannot be understood without examining the interaction between the judicial and the political arenas – as Reva Siegel has shown in her article on that decision (2023).

The *Dobbs* conflict is an appropriate place to end this section, because it combined the mechanisms of legal mobilization, the social construction of basic elements of American life, changes in institutional and contingent opportunity structures, and on a movement-countermovement interaction. In Section 5, we will employ these four mechanisms to analyze two other areas of legal and social movement scholarship: the development of marriage equality in the United States and the rise and development of the "social constitution" in South Africa.

5 Two Test Cases

In this section of the Element, we apply the four intersecting mechanisms that we proposed in Section 4 – *legal mobilization, social construction of the law, political/legal opportunity structure, and movement/countermovement interaction* – as a framework for examining the relations between law and social movements to two very different cases: the struggle to legalize same-sex marriage in the United States and the rise of social constitutionalism in South Africa. We do not challenge the findings and approaches of other scholars to this intersection – in fact, we build on them – but we think these four mechanisms, especially when combined, hold promise to advance the fusion we seek to advance.

5.1 The Chequered History of Same-Sex Marriage in the United States[41]

On May 18, 1970, James McConnell, a librarian, and Richard Baker, a law student at the University of Minnesota, applied for a marriage license in

---

[39] 505 U.S. 833 (1992).   [40] 597 U.S. (2022).
[41] The following passages rely heavily on Dorf and Tarrow (2013) and on Fetner (2008).

Minneapolis. When the request was denied on the ground that the couple were of the same sex, they filed a suit in district court to force the state to take action on the grounds that the refusal to grant their request violated the First, Eighth, Ninth, and Fourteenth Amendments of the Constitution. When the court denied their petition, the couple took their case to the Minnesota Supreme Court, which unanimously affirmed the trial court's dismissal.[42] When the plaintiffs took the case to the US Supreme Court, the Justices issued a one-sentence order sustaining the Minnesota court's decision on the grounds that the appeal did not raise a substantial federal question.

Now fast-forward 45 years to June 26, 2015, when, in a 5–4 decision, the Supreme Court ruled, in the case of *Obergefell* v. *Hodges*,[43] that the fundamental right to marry is guaranteed to same-sex couples by both the Due Process Clause and the Equal Protection Clause of the Fourteenth Amendment. *Obergefell* followed by two years the case of *United States* v. *Windsor*.[44] In that case, a widow, Edith Windsor, had married a woman named Thea Spyer in Canada. When Spyer passed away, the IRS insisted on taxing Windsor on her estate on the grounds that the two women were not legally married in the United States, where the Defense of Marriage Act (DOMA), had defined marriage to be limited to the union of one man and one woman.[45]

District Courts leading to *Obergefell* had ruled for a group of same-sex couples who claimed the right to marry. Judges in the Fourth, Seventh, Ninth, and Tenth Circuits had held that state-level bans on same-sex marriage were unconstitutional, but the Sixth Circuit, on appeal, ruled that it was bound by *Baker* v. *Nelson,* leading to the Supreme Court review in *Obergefell.* In a decision written by the Court's swing Justice, Anthony Kennedy, the Court focused on the "evolving understanding" of discrimination and inequality in the United States and deliberately overturned *Baker* (Eskridge and Spedale 2007: 20–23).

"Evolving understanding" was putting it mildly! In the years since *Baker* v. *Nelson,* a series of episodes both in and outside of the courts ate at what the courts in Minneapolis had so confidently regarded as settled law. But this "understanding" evolved by fits and starts, advances and retreats, and by some advances that were originally seen as defeats (NeJaime 2011). An early advance followed by defeat was made in the State of Hawaii when, in the case of *Baehr* v. *Lewin*[46] three same-sex couples sued the state on the basis of the state's

---

[42] 29 *Minn.* 310, 191 N.W.2d 185 (1971). See Eskridge and Spedale (2007).
[43] 576 U.S. 644 (2015).   [44] 570 U.S. 744 (2013).
[45] The Defense of Marriage Act (DOMA) was passed by the 104th Congress in 1995–6 as Public Law 104.
[46] 75 Haw. 530 (1993).

constitutional provision guaranteeing equal protection. The State Supreme Court sent the case back to a lower court, but before that court could rule on the constitutional issue, the legislature passed a law limiting marriage to opposite-sex couples and the voters amended the state constitution to make clear that the legislature had the right to impose such a law.

Baehr sent a ripple of concern among LGBTQ activists across the country, who had put marriage was on the back burner out of fear that focusing on it would trigger successful opposition on the Right (Stone 2012). Their fears were realized when, Congress, in 1996, passed DOMA, soon followed by fifteen states. For the remainder of the decade, the initiative lay with the anti-gay marriage movement, as Figure 1 shows.

Same-sex marriage advocates scored a partial victory in 1999 when the Vermont Supreme Court invalidated that state's opposite-sex-only-marriage-only law in the case of *Baker* v. *State*.[47] But although the gay rights movement had carefully prepared the ground in Vermont before filing suit, the state legislature opted for legalizing civil unions and not marriage (Klarman 2013:

LEGEND

■   Defines marriage as relationship between a man and a women

▣   State DOMA law but allows civil unions or domestic partnership

■   States with statute or judicial decision allowing same sex-marriage

Figure 1 States with DOMA Laws as of 2013

Source: www.pewresearch.org/religion/2015/06/26/same-sex-marriage-state-by-state-1/.

---

[47] 744 A.2d 864 (Vt. 1999).

77–83). As the controversy inched up between different courts, various states, and involved judges, advocacy groups of different complexions, and different facts of the case, the meaning of marriage was reshaped, leading to the evolution of key political figures like then-Vice President Joseph Biden and, eventually, President Barack Obama.

The advantage shifted more decisively to the LGBTQ movement in the wake of two decisions of the Supreme Court that did *not* involve marriage. In a 1996 opinion, the Court made a first pro-gay-rights ruling in the case of, *Romer* v. *Evans*.[48] In *Romer*, the Court invalidated a state constitutional amendment enacted by referendum on the ground that, in forbidding all levels of government in Colorado from adopting laws protecting gays and lesbians against sexual orientation discrimination, the voters had acted out of "animus" in violation of the federal Fourteenth Amendment.

Then, in 2003, in the case of *Lawrence* v. *Texas*,[49] the Court invalidated a criminal statute that forbade "sodomy" when performed by people of the same sex. Police had received a report of weapons in an apartment, but when they broke into the apartment, they found two men engaged in sexual activity. Drawing on a state anti-sodomy law, the two individuals were booked for indecent activity. Justice Anthony Kennedy's opinion, like his earlier one in *Romer,* did not expressly say that same-sex intimacy was a fundamental right akin to freedom of speech, but he left little doubt that his (and the Court's) sympathies was moving in the direction of protection for same-sex couples.

Later that year, the Massachusetts Supreme Judicial Court relied on the logic of *Lawrence* 'in the case of *Goodridge* v. *Department of Public Health*,[50] gave recognition to same-sex marriage. Soon after, three state courts followed the example of *Goodridge* by finding a right to same-sex marriage under their state constitutions. After Goodridge, when public opinion had already turned in favor of same-sex marriage, courts in California and Connecticut and Iowa found a right to it.[51] Soon after, legislatures in three other states and in the District of Columbia made same-sex marriage legal.[52] As the logic of

---

[48] 517 US 620 (1996), establishing that homosexuals, lesbians, and bisexuals possess the same rights as any group of persons to seek governmental protection against discrimination.

[49] 539 US 558 (2003), establishing that most sanctions of criminal punishment for consensual, adult non-procreative sexual activity (commonly referred to as sodomy laws) are unconstitutional.

[50] 798 N.E.2d 941 (Mass. 2003), in which the Massachusetts Supreme Judicial Court held that the Massachusetts Constitution requires the state to legally recognize same-sex marriage.

[51] In California in the *In re Marriage Cases*; in Connecticut in *Kerrigan* v. *Commissioner of Public Health* and in Iowa in *Varnum* v. *Brien*.

[52] The decisions in Maine and Vermont came in 2009; in New Hampshire, New York, and the District of Columbia in 2010.

Goodridge diffused, there was a wave of same-sex marriages in San Francisco and in other cities.[53]

In 2008, California passed a referendum ("Prop 8"), put forward by a well-funded anti-gay marriage coalition. But this proposition was overturned by a district court in 2010, a ruling that the US Court of Appeals for the Ninth Circuit affirmed in the case of *Perry* v. *Brown*.[54] The US Supreme Court then held that the state's refusal to defend Prop 8 had rendered the appeals court without jurisdiction, which had the effect of leaving the ruling of the district court in place.

The Prop 8 conflict had the unexpected result of producing a split within the LGBTQ movement in California between the major gay rights and civil liberties groups and a new organization, AFER, which "assembled expert litigation teams." These teams, wrote NeJaime (2012: 662–3), "can rely on the vast resources and professional staff of their large, national law firms." Led by nationally prominent lawyers, Ted Olson and David Boies, they took to the airwaves and received favorable coverage from high-profile print media.

However, it was the national court system that increasingly took the initiative away from the states. On the same day as it invalidated Prop 8, a different Supreme Court majority left standing a lower court opinion without reaching the merits. Writing for the Court, Justice Kennedy wrote eloquently of the equal dignity to which same-sex couples are entitled but recognized the power of the states with respect to defining marriage. Paired with the ruling in the Prop 8 case, the Court's opinion with respect to DOMA indicated that while a majority of the justices were sympathetic to the cause of same-sex marriage, they were not yet ready to guarantee it a nationwide right.

In 2013, same-sex marriage turned the corner in the states. On January 1, same-sex marriage was made legal in Maryland. Rhode Island, Delaware, Minnesota, Hawaii, and Illinois. Later that year, two federal district court rulings legalized same-sex marriage, at least pending appellate consideration. Reading the results of these developments, but also under pressure from increasingly assertive LGBTQ advocates, members of the political elite – as well as members of the mass public – began to turn in favor of same-sex marriage (Hunter 2017).

Consider the "evolution" of President Barack Obama. In 2004, he had declared that marriage was "between a man and a woman"; in the 2008

---

[53] Even in conservative San Diego, gay demonstrators conducted a "kiss-in" outside a hotel whose owners had donated support for Prop 8 (Klarman 2013: 125).

[54] 671 F.3d 1052 (9th circuit, 2014). The most detailed analysis of Prop 8 and its intersection with movement strategies and court decisions comes from NeJaime, in his "The Legal Mobilization Dilemma" (2012), especially Section III of that article.

campaign for the Presidency, his position moved to support for civil unions; but early in 2012, he voiced support for same-sex marriage, a historic first for an American president. By the time the Supreme Court heard oral arguments in *Obergefell*, fifty-four senators, 180 members of the House of Representatives, fifteen governors, and at least 117 mayors had declared themselves for legalizing same-sex marriage. These advances were driven by the four processes we outlined in Section 4.

5.1.1 Legal Mobilization

One way to tell the story of the recognition of same-sex marriage would be to outline the actions and the strategies of the formal organizations that represented same-sex clients in court, organized state-level referenda both for and against recognition, lobbied state and federal officials, and ran educational and protest campaigns.[55] A variant of this approach would be to measure the dramatic growth in the financial bases of these organizations, as Michael Klarman did in his *From the Closet to the Altar.* The number of gay and lesbian advocacy groups continued to grow and gain more resources during the two decades following *Baehr.* In the vanguard was "Lambda Legal: "Between 1983 and 1992," writes Klarman (2013: 70–1), "Lambda Legal's annual income rose from $133,000 to $1.6 million, and its paid staff increased from three to twenty-two."

Not only did traditional advocacy groups like Lambda take up the cause of LGBTQ marriage rights after Prop 8; new and more aggressive organizations, like Freedom to Marry, appeared on the scene, nourished by the financial clout of some sectors of the gay and lesbian community (Cummings and NeJaime 2010: 1307). While we cannot directly connect particular spurts in support to particular junctures in the history of the marriage campaign, we do find a sharp uptick in support for LGBTQ advocacy groups among elites from the mid-1990s on.

But few advocacy groups gain purchase in the absence of a mass base. These not only form the shock troops for their actions but also represent groups of "apolitical" people who provide small donations, occasionally attend rallies, and show by example that their relationships do not represent a threat. Unlike historical movements that depended on outward expressions of outrage, the movement for same-sex marriage was empowered by many people whose lives together spurred collective action by the activist minority. In other words, it was

---

[55] A vigorous critic of the role of professional LGBTQ organizations in the campaign for same-sex marriage is Dean Spade, who argued that as movements professionalize and upper-class people take the reins and set the agenda, a shift happens toward an individual rights framework, which led inexorably to the right to marry. For Spade's views, see his essay *Marriage Will Never Set Us Free* with Craig Willse (2015).

the *interaction* between the mass and elite levels of the gay and lesbian communities that produced the legal mobilization that produced the progress reported above.

In the course of their interviews with leaders of the same-sex marriage movement, Dorf and Tarrow became aware of the role of ordinary people who previously had not thought much – if at all – about same-sex marriage, and who now started thinking about it. As one elite respondent told them, "In the early 90s, it began to change. At the end of the day, it's about the people and people were lining up to get their licenses . . . It was like people lining up for grain." Several of Dorf and Tarrow's (2014: 465–6) respondents implicitly or explicitly criticized LGBTQ movement organizations for their unwillingness to take up the controversial issue of marriage sooner. As one respondent put it:

> The LGBT organizations were NOT in the vanguard, grassroots groups were in the vanguard. . . . The legal groups said it was a bad idea, with the exception of a group in Hollywood. It was grassroots groups that led the way.

As they concluded from their survey of movement leaders:

> . . .spurred by the onslaught of federal and state discriminatory legislation and constitutional enactment, increasing numbers of same-sex couples at the grassroots level – some of them with substantial financial resources – began to pressure the LGBT movement – which had previously shied away from the issue of marriage – to go to court and to mount electoral referenda against the growing tide of legislation and constitutional amendments privileging opposite-sex unions. (460–1)

Legal mobilization was the outcome of the activation of ordinary gay couples and the pressure they put on elite advocacy groups.

5.1.2 The Social (Re)Construction of Marriage

Despite the progress made on gay rights by the early 1990s, "until the turn of the century," writes Klarman (2013: 45), "the idea that same-sex couples should be legally permitted to marry would have struck most Americans as ludicrous. In 1991, roughly 75 percent of Americans still thought that same-sex sodomy was morally wrong . . . Opinion polls conducted around 1990 showed support for gay marriage between 11 percent and 23 percent." But opinion polls were slowly beginning to show growing support for the right of gays and lesbians to adopt children. "In turn," notes Klarman, "once same-sex couples were permitted to adopt children, explaining why these couples should not be permitted to marry became much harder." No surprise, then that the percentage of Americans who thought same-sex marriage was "always wrong" declined from between 70 and 80 percent in the 1970s and 1980s to below 60 percent by the turn of the century (70).

Changes in popular culture helped to bring about this change. During the first two decades after *Baehr* there was a sharp uptick in the appearance of the terms "same-sex marriage" and "gay marriage" in book publications, while the use of the more traditional term "homosexual marriage" remained virtually flat. This linguistic change was accompanied by the normalization of same-sex relationships in popular culture, especially on television, where gay characters began to be portrayed as fundamentally no different from straight ones on sitcoms like *Will and Grace*. A slow but steady social re-construction of the meaning of marriage lay behind the overt legal mobilization of elite advocates and their supporters. But none of this would have come to fruition in the absence of changes in the opportunity structure.

5.1.3 Using the Political-Legal Opportunity Structure

We see changes in the political-legal opportunity structure as being largely responsible for shaping the interactions between advocates for marriage equality and traditional marriage forces. Two factors traditional associated with political opportunity stand out: changes in movement strategy as the result of changes in popular culture concerning the nature of marriage; and the interaction between movement and countermovement actors in the course of the conflict over same-sex marriage. In terms of the three core features of legal opportunity that Lisa Vanahla identifies – legal stock, standing, and rules on cost – changes in legal stock were most important – namely, changes in the legal architecture of Supreme Court decisions.

Three examples will show how key court decisions (which reshaped the legal stock and then reshaped movement and countermovement dynamics) had an impact on the political-legal opportunity structure of both the LGBTQ community and on its opponents:

First, Baehr both put marriage on the agenda of a reluctant movement and panicked the antigay religious right (Stone 2012: 31).

Second, Romer "discouraged the right from trying to pass broadly antigay laws, leading opponents of gay rights to turn to the narrower ground of opposing same-sex marriage, while encouraging the LGBTQ movement to believe that the courts might sustain more gay-friendly equal protection cases" (Dorf and Tarrow 2014: 461).

Third, Lawrence declared that it was not the business of a state to forbid same-sex relationships between consenting adults (Dorf and Tarrow 2014: 462).

But it was not only in the courts that the political opportunity structure opened for same-sex marriage. Decisions by public officials, like Mayor Gavin Newsom of San Francisco and Mayor Jason West of New Paltz, to open their city halls to gay and lesbian marriages sent an important message to advocates in the movement. Also relevant – because he was what one interviewee called "a consummate political opportunist" – was Governor Andrew Cuomo's role who appointed gay civil servants to high positions in the state administration and pushed through the state's Marriage Equality Act in 2011 (462).[56]

Not only were political elites beginning to come around to support for same-sex marriage; worried about losing their firms' ability to attract talented employees to their states – elites in the business community began to lobby for the reform. As early as 1991, *Fortune* reported that gays were "coming out of the closet in corporate America," forming gay employee associations and pushing for non-discrimination policies, diversity training, and domestic partnership benefits" (Klarman 2013: 41).

As attitudes shifted, the movement gained ground in the institutions of civil society to (Hunter 2017). The US Conference of Mayors "became the first organization of elected officials in the United States to support civil rights protections for gays and lesbians at all levels of government," notes Klarman (2013: 41–2). By the end of the 1980s, more than sixty cities had enacted similar reforms. This type of support put the cause of gay Americans within the gates of American politics. The shift, however, was double-edged. Support from businesses and elected politicians helped to legitimate the movement; but on the other hand, when politicians sensed that their constituents were not ready to accept gay marriage, they could turn away from the cause on a dime. The movement's adoption of marriage as a central goal was also spurred by external pressure, in a process of movement-countermovement interaction, as we argue below.

5.1.4 Movement-Countermovement Interaction

In looking to the future in his 2013 book on the progress of same-sex marriage. Klarman (2013: 157) noted that "*Despite the backlash against gay marriage* in Maine and Iowa in 2009–10, the overall trend toward liberalization of attitudes and policies on gay rights issues remained unmistakable" (emphasis added). It was certainly the case that public and elite opinion were shifting dramatically in favor of same-sex marriage when Klarman wrote, but before this occurred, there

---

[56] On Newsom's and West's role, see Klarman (2013: 189–91). On Cuomo's role in pushing through marriage equality in New York State, see Klarman (2013: 71).

was a process of what Dorf and Tarrow called "anticipatory mobilization." By this term, these authors meant that – apart from *Baehr* and a few other scattered cases – the countermovement to the same-sex marriage campaign mobilized before the movement vigorously took up the cause. But, in doing so, it spurred popular support for the reform which pushed movement elites to take up the cause.

Of course, the movement-countermovement cycle that we traced above was presaged by the *Baehr* case, but as Klarman and others make clear, that case was an isolated one. Initiated by three Hawaiian couples and supported by the local branch of the ACLU, it did not enjoy the support of either the national ACLU or any of the national LGBTQ groups, which worried that it would trigger a backlash against the movement as a whole. They were largely correct, but it was the religious right's "anticipatory mobilization" to *Baehr* that forced the LGBTQ movement to take up the issue of marriage (Dorf and Tarrow 2014: 450).

The dynamic of a cycle of contention initiated by a countermovement has been recognized by other scholars who have worked on sexual politics. In his careful analysis of the California case of *Perry* v. *Brown,* NeJaime showed how the early success of the same-sex marriage movement triggered the rise of a deep-pocketed anti-gay marriage movement, which led to a successful "Yes on 8" movement that produced a success for the proposition with fifty-two percent of the vote (NeJaime 2012: 707). As Tina Fetner (2008: 112) writes: "Leaders in the religious right may have thought the issue of marriage would be an easy victory, given how important the symbolic aspects of marriage are to many people." And, indeed, through the first decade of this century, the religious right won most of the electoral battles it fought.

But the campaign for same-sex marriage led to a widespread sympathy for same-sex couples – what NeJaime calls the "mainstreaming of marriage equality" – and LGBTQ equality more generally (714). In this case, legal mobilization attracted the support of elites, influenced the political opportunity structure, and led to a slow but steady shift in the opinion of both judges and state legislatures.

To summarize: Although the visible high points in the success of the same-sex marriage campaign lay in the courts, those court decisions cannot be understood only by the legal mobilization of the LGBTQ movement; it was threatened by a militant countermovement and was pushed forward by ordinary gay and lesbian couples at the grassroots. The combination of the opening of the legal-political opportunity structure and the changing social construction of marriage provided the incentives and resources for both elite and mass-level actions on behalf of a reform which – only a few decades earlier – had seemed most unlikely to succeed. The strategic move of the *anti*-same-sex marriage lobby, passing marriage laws at both the federal and state levels and using state-level referenda to mobilize its conservative base, triggered a once-reluctant social movement to take action on behalf of same-sex marriage.

5.2 Social Constitutionalism in South Africa

Before turning to social constitutionalism in South Africa, we need to make clear what this term means. Brinks, Gauri, and Shen (2015: 290) define this form of constitutionalism as "the increasing inclusion of social and economic rights language in constitutions, the increasing use of that language by social actors to pursue their goals, and the increasing judicialization of political disputes under the social rights rubric." Constitutions that fall within this model include expansive rights protections and broad review powers for the judiciary. Most of the constitutional reforms of the late 1980s through the early 2000s – which occurred across Latin America, sub-Saharan Africa, Europe, and Asia – implicate some sense of social constitutionalism. Figure 2 shows the change in the number of constitutions that recognize the rights to health, housing, an adequate standard of living, and/or social security over time.

At times, this shift in the function of constitutional law has been accompanied by the creation of mechanisms to allow citizens to claim their rights with relative ease. The rights implicated in social constitutionalism encompass not

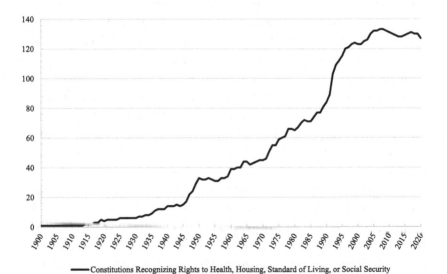

Constitutions Recognizing Rights to Health, Housing, Standard of Living, or Social Security

Figure 2 Constitutions recognizing social rights over time

Source: Comparative Constitutions Project (Elkins and Ginsburg 2021).

only the most immediate provisions necessary to make participation in political and social life theoretically possible (e.g., the right to assemble or the right to vote), but also those provisions necessary to make participation in social and political life actually feasible (e.g., access to healthcare, housing, and education).[57]

South Africa's political system featured long-standing parliamentary sovereignty and a legal system that at once served to implement the structures of apartheid but also provided tools for occasional successes in the fight against it. As Meierhenrich (2008: 142) observes, "Black South Africans could not be voters under apartheid, but they could be plaintiffs – and successful plaintiffs at that."[58] With resistance to apartheid coming to a head in the late 1980s, the sense that a fundamental change in the structure of the state was necessary prevailed. During the negotiated transition to democratic rule in the middle of the 1990s, members of the constitutional assembly adopted a new social constitution. The next few paragraphs detail the early constitutional history of South Africa and the events leading up to the adoption of social constitutionalism.

In 1909, the South Africa Act codified the creation of the Union of South Africa, unifying four settler states in the process. This move solidified the geographic and political bifurcation of white and non-white South Africans at the recommendations of the Lagden Commission. Around this time, a group of white delegates met at the National Convention to determine the future of the Cape, Natal, Transvaal, and Orange River colonies, as well as the status of non-white South Africans in the new united South Africa. These colonies had separately developed distinct constitutional traditions (Dugard 1990). The resulting 1910 Constitution of the Union of South Africa had many features of Westminster-based constitutions; however, it also included severe limitations on the franchise.

In 1948, the National Party came to power and implemented a series of laws further distinguishing between the rights of South Africans of different races, establishing the apartheid system. Throughout this period, the constitutional order remained the same, while the state became both more and more exclusionary and more and more interventionist (particularly through efforts to create and maintain so-called "homelands" as well as the system of pass laws[59]). In 1996, South Africa adopted a new, "final" constitution that fit the social constitutionalist model.[60]

---

[57] See discussions in Brinks, Gauri, and Shen (2015) and Taylor (2023b).

[58] On the double-edged nature of pre-transition South African constitutionalism, see Abel (1995).

[59] For more on the pass law system specifically, see Abel (1995). For a detailed history of homelands or "Bantustans," see Phillips (2017).

[60] In 1993, South Africa adopted an "Interim Constitution" that was replaced by the "Final Constitution" of 1996.

Social movements played a key role in setting the stage for this epochal shift. Anti-apartheid activists took part in robust debates about what exactly the future of the country should look like and the kinds of political and legal structures that ought to shape that future. Most notable among these movements was the African National Congress (ANC). Whereas the ANC started out drawing relatively conservative members, by the 1940s, the left-leaning ANC Youth League led by Nelson Mandela, Walter Sisulu, and Oliver Tambo, had gained prominence in the organization (Lodge 1983). Throughout the 1950s, ANC membership grew significantly, and the movement relied on mass protests, boycotts, and strikes to contest apartheid policies. In April 1960, the apartheid government banned the ANC, driving much of the movement's leadership underground or into exile. In 1961, following the Sharpeville massacre, the ANC developed into a hybrid organization that featured a military offshoot, Umkhonto we Sizwe (MK). While MK engaged in violent attacks, the ANC continued to pursue non-violent tactics, such as protests and legal claims, as well.[61]

In 1955, the ANC, along with the other members of the anti-apartheid coalition known as the Congress Alliance, drafted the Freedom Charter at the Congress of the People in Kliptown, which set out a vision of an inclusive, rights-protective state ruled by and for the people. This vision is one that is consistent with the social constitutionalist model, though social constitutionalism as such did not yet exist. As Abel (1995: 14) writes, the Freedom Charter, "contains an enumeration of rights that have furnished critical criteria and a blueprint for the post-apartheid society for nearly half a century." The ANC solicited input from residents of both townships and rural areas, and the Congress of the People involved nearly three thousand delegates (Mandela 1995: 170–6). Ultimately, the Freedom Charter included demands for democracy, equality before the law, human rights protections, access to land and work, education, housing, and peace (though not social constitutions per se). The Freedom Charter impacted the organization of the resistance movement.

In 1959, the Pan-African Congress split off from the ANC, citing displeasure with the Freedom Charter as one of its primary rationales for the move. Further, the Freedom Charter later impacted the policy platform of the ANC as the country transitioned out of apartheid. In fact, the ANC adapted the Freedom Charter into a document entitled "Ready to Govern," and it featured heavily in the ANC's policy platforms as it began to lead the country.

---

[61] For more on the anti-apartheid struggle, see the ANC's "Strategy and Tactics" (1994) policy documents, as well as Mandela (1995) and Sparks (1996).

Throughout the 1960s and 1970s, even as apartheid deepened, the debate about constitutional law widened, particularly with respect to the inclusion of a Bill of Rights. Specifically, an opposition party known as the Progressive Party routinely pressed for the addition of a bill of rights to the South African constitution. In 1960, following the advice of the Molteno Commission, the Progressive Party adopted the policy goal of drafting a bill of rights. Members of the United Party also voiced support for this proposal. In the following year, the country left the Commonwealth, developing a new constitution and renaming itself the Republic of South Africa. This new constitution did not bring with it the addition of rights recognitions or the possibility of judicial review. Instead, the white-dominated Parliament continued to rein supreme,[62] passing new national security laws that allowed for detention without trial and abolishing habeas corpus protections.

In 1973, as Dugard (2015: 48) recalls, "a group of South Africans of all races, comprising most black leaders, Progressive Party representatives, newspaper editors, and academics, adopted a declaration of consensus which proposed that 'the rights of each individual be protected by a bill of rights entrenched in the federal constitution.'" Popular calls for consideration of a bill of rights continued to grow through the early 1980s. Yet, the 1983 Tricameral Constitution did not feature either judicial review or a bill of rights.

While the legal system before the end of apartheid was profoundly discriminatory and the modal legal system official did nothing to challenge it, certain judges did offer rights-protective positions that provided toeholds for anti-apartheid activists. Further, a robust group of anti-apartheid lawyers emerged, forming public interest organizations, such as the Legal Resource Centre, the Black Sash, the Centre for Applied Legal Studies, the Treason Trial Defense Fund, and the South African Defense and Aid Fund. Abel (1995), in particular, documents how lawyers, activists, and ordinary South Africans engaged in legal campaigns against pass laws, conscription, unfair labor practices, torture, and other abuse of prisoners, among other things.

Further, as Meierhenrich (2008: 4) holds, the system conformed to specific legal principles, which despite their myriad flaws established the foundation necessary for a relatively peaceful transition. He notes, "in apartheid's endgame, the memory of formally rational law – and agents' confidence in its past

---

[62] The Bantu Authorities Act of 1951 established separate governing structures for the Black population and the Indian population living in South Africa had not been granted the right to vote, while the ruling National Party attempted to disenfranchise the Coloured in various ways throughout the 1950s. Between 1956 and 1969, the Separate Representation of Voters Act allowed Coloured voters to elect four members of Parliament. Starting in 1969, only white voters were enfranchised.

and future utility in the transition from authoritarian rule – created the conditions for the emergence of trust between democracy-demanding and democracy-resisting elites." In other words, a shared belief in the idea of law allowed these otherwise diametrically opposed elites to negotiate together the end of apartheid and the start of democratic rule.

Constitutional negotiations took place between 1990 and 1993, and they included the Conventions for a Democratic South Africa (CODESA I and II) and the Multi-Party Negotiating Process (MPNP). The resulting Interim Constitution of 1993 introduced judicial review, created a Constitutional Court, and established a Bill of Rights. This Bill of Rights did not include robust social rights protections, but neither did it preclude them from being added later in the Final Constitution, which is precisely what occurred.

The remainder of this section details the consequences of social constitutionalism, with reference to the four processes identified above: the political-legal opportunity structure, legal mobilization, the social construction of meanings of rights and law, and movement/countermovement dynamics. These four processes are fundamentally intertwined.

5.2.1 The Political-Legal Opportunity Structure

The introduction of new constitutions fundamentally reshaped the political-legal opportunity structure in South Africa. Recall that the following features comprise the political opportunity structure: "access to the formal institutional structure, availability of allies, the configuration of power with respect to relevant issues/challengers," and "the underlying political culture." The existence of a new constitution and a type of new constitutionalism reflected a shift in what Andersen (2005) identifies as "the underlying political culture."

The constitution-drafting process was billed in South Africa as a "refounding" moment, one that would mark the start of a more equitable country and a move away from old, exclusionary modes of politics. New rounds of elections, as well as the creation of new institutions (e.g., "Chapter 9 Institutions" including the Human Rights Commission), meant changes in access to formal institutional structures, and new potential allies for social movement actors in both elected and unelected positions of power. This new political culture was informed by a sense of a shared constitutional project on the part of the Constitutional Court and the executive branch, controlled by the ANC.

This vision seems to have set out the parameters for inter-branch relations in South Africa, at least through the presidencies of Nelson Mandela and Thabo Mbeki. As Fowkes (2016: 70) meticulously documents, early Constitutional

Court decisions reflected an effort to "start as actors jointly working to build a new and better system – an utterly defining, and widely neglected, feature of the post-1994 South African polity." Fowkes refers to this as a "constitution-building approach," in which judges weigh the costs and benefits of intervention not only against their preferences, the likelihood of an immediately desirable outcome, or the political survival of the institution. Instead, judges considered also "the building work that can be done by letting other institutions do their jobs and by expressing trust in them" (70). Thus, the new institutional framework empowered the Constitutional Court, but the Constitutional Court under the guidance of Judge President Arthur Chaskalson also sought to avoid unnecessary conflicts with the executive branch.

Turning now to the core features of legal opportunity: *legal stock, standing rules, and rules on costs*, as laid out by Vanhala, South Africa's new constitution immediately recognized all enumerated rights as justiciable, including social rights. Rather than creating a new legal mechanism to expand access to rights, the South African Constitution lowered standing requirements, as described in Article 38. These lower standing requirements allow individuals not directly affected by a rights violation to file claims on behalf of those who are so affected. Further, though most constitutional claims must begin at the High Court level, under certain conditions, claimants can directly petition the Constitutional Court, asking the Court to serve as the first and last instance because of the urgency of the issue in question, though this direct access mechanism has been used quite infrequently. In fact, the Constitutional Court has also chosen to limit direct access to the Court, preferring to allow lower courts to hear cases first, though the appeals process can draw cases out for years, potentially limiting the impact of rights decisions for individual claimants (Dugard 2006, 2015). The development and restriction of direct access demonstrates how legal opportunity can appear open on paper, but actually be quite closed in practice.

5.2.2 Legal Mobilization

The new opportunity structure facilitated new patterns of legal mobilization. Most clearly, claims to social rights (rights that had not been recognized previously) increased significantly. Citizens, NGOs, and – especially – social movements experimented with using the new constitutional framework, bringing different kinds of claims and legal arguments before the Constitutional Court. The South African Constitutional Court heard an average of just under three social rights cases each year between 1996 and 2016. Of these cases, the majority dealt with the right to housing. In fact, as of 2016, the Court had decided thirty-one housing rights cases, compared to fifteen education rights cases, five social security cases, seven health cases, and two cases involving water.

Social movements were integral to two of the most notable of these cases, the *Treatment Action Campaign* case of 2002[63] and the KZN Slums Act case. The Treatment Action Campaign (TAC) was a social movement founded by Zackie Achmat, an HIV-positive activist, which went to court to demand that a reluctant government be required to roll out a full program to distribute the antiretroviral drugs to all expecting mothers, rather than simply pilot the program at a few medical facilities. The TAC won its case, suggesting that post-Apartheid South Africa was not going to leave its social movement past behind.

Second, in the "KZN Slums Act" case,[64] a group called Abahlali baseMjondolo successfully halted the planned eviction of shack-dwellers in the province of KwaZulu-Natal. Abahlali baseMjondolo (a name that means "residents of the shacks" in isiZulu) is a shack-dwellers' movement that was founded in 2005. The movement relies on protests, land occupations, and litigation to pursue land reform, the protection of housing rights, and the provision of basic services for shack dwellers.[65]

Overall, social rights cases make up about 9 percent of the Court's work – a not insignificant percentage. These decisions have had major impacts on housing policy (e.g., the conditions under which evictions may take place and the duties of the state to provide "alternative accommodation" for those facing evictions), healthcare policy (e.g., the rollout of a plan to provide of anti-retroviral medications to HIV-infected mothers across the country), and education policy (e.g., the updating of school infrastructure away from mud schools).

5.2.3 Social (Re)construction of Rights

Not only did the emergence of social constitutionalism reshape the political-legal opportunity structure and facilitate new patterns in legal mobilization in South Africa; it also allowed for the development of new understandings of rights. As they engaged in the process of filing and deciding legal claims, claimants, activists, and judges expanded the meaning of particular rights as they engaged in the process of filing and deciding legal claims.

---

[63] *Minister of Health and Others* v. *Treatment Action Campaign and Others.* 2002. www.saflii.org/za/cases/ZACC/2002/15.html.

[64] *Abahlali baseMjondolo Movement SA and Another* v. *Premier of the Province of Kwazulu-Natal and Others.* 2009. www.saflii.org/za/cases/ZACC/2009/31.html.

[65] See Abahlali's webpage: https://abahlali.org/.

Housing rights provides a window into how such expansions occurred. In the 2000 *Grootboom* decision,[66] the Constitutional Court found that the state's housing policy was "unreasonable," and therefore unconstitutional, because it did not include sufficient provisions for those "in desperate need," like Irene Grootboom and the 900 others who had been displaced by flooding. The state – ultimately unconvincingly – argued that it had limited funds to address the housing crisis and that the Court should not second-guess its housing policy decisions.

The *Grootboom* decision set off a chain of cases that were related to the right to housing in the context of evictions. One former clerk who went on to work for an NGO and litigate housing rights cases described the development of the right to housing as follows:

> Under apartheid, it was illegal to be a squatter, and you could be kicked out and you could be thrown in jail . . . [Now] you [can] evict someone, but only with a court order, and only if it's equitable . . . Built into the right is if eviction is going to lead to homelessness, the state must provide you with temporary alternative accommodation. And over the past 20 years, that has been expanded. It's not just if you're a flood victim the state must provide this accommodation, it's also if the state evicts you. Then the next step is when the state evicts you from private land. Then the next step, if a private owner evicts you, also you have this right. And now we're getting to the content of what that alternative accommodation looks like . . . So, we're seeing – and what's so lovely and unexpected – is the Court has started writing case law on this, kind of like a handbook for litigators . . . The jurisprudence has developed to such a level that the courts are now writing, "Judges, when they decide this issue, have to do X, Y, Z."[67]

Thus, there has been a steady expansion of the legal scope of the right to housing, built step-by-step, from emergency or crisis protections to more everyday protections. One lawyer explained, "in housing, the area where there's been the greatest success is that evictions have been made very much more difficult through the Constitution and through very skilled and energetic lawyers who had pushed the boundaries of the Constitution beyond what anyone imagined at the time it was written."[68]

What's more, Abahlali baseMjondolo, the social movement organized by shack-dwellers mentioned above, has adopted rights-based language in contesting evictions. Abahlali has posters that detail the steps necessary for evictions to proceed lawfully posted in their offices, and members are well-versed in the

---

[66] *Government of the Republic of South Africa and Others* v. *Grootboom and Others*. 2000. www .saflii.org/za/cases/ZACC/2000/19.html.

[67] Interview, August 28, 2017. Johannesburg, South Africa.

[68] Interview, March 27, 2018. Cape Town, South Africa.

intricacies of housing rights provisions and relevant laws. The issue of housing – especially as it relates to evictions – has been thoroughly judicialized in the South African context, with housing understood through the lens of law, and both social and legal understandings of the right to housing expanding over time.

5.2.4 Movement-Countermovement Interaction

In South Africa, social movements were highly influential at various moments for the adoption and development of social constitutionalism. The section above detailed the importance of the anti-apartheid movement, especially the early commitment of movement actors to the Freedom Charter with its emphasis on both "freedom and bread," or civil and political *and* social and economic rights. The ANC's strategy was not without internal opponents. Even in the 1950s, there had been disagreement among resistance groups, with the Pan African Congress splintering from the ANC, in part due to disagreements regarding the Freedom Charter. Skipping ahead several decades, as social constitutionalism came to be adopted, the business community began to feel threatened by this new legal environment. As an expert advisor on the Technical Committee remembered:

> [A]t the point of the Constitutional Assembly, there wasn't really active opposition coming to their inclusion [social and economic rights] from NGO groups but at that time of the certification of the Constitution there was then an objection from groups like the Free Market Foundation . . . But, you know, they didn't make very active submissions at that time of the drafting of the Constitution.[69]

Arguably, these business-oriented actors missed their opportunity to influence the new constitutional order. It might have been much easier to contest the constitutional recognition of social and economic rights during the constitutional assembly, a period of time during which a much more liberal constitution (the Interim Constitution of 1993) prevailed. Once these rights were recognized, and once specific actors were empowered to adjudicate them, it became less likely that relatively limited, factionalized contestation would lead to their dismissal.

Later, other movements and interest groups came to contest the new constitution on additional grounds. As Heinz Klug (2016: 48) describes it, "there is increasing criticism of what is perceived to be the 'liberal' legal order created by the historic transition from apartheid and now blamed for its failure to address

---

[69] Interview, May 14, 2018. Cape Town, South Africa.

the legacies of racism and economic inequality that survived the democratic transition." These views target the 1996 Constitution as the centerpiece of the incomplete transition: "Unhappiness at the slow pace of social change and growing inequality has led both government and opposition parties to blame the Constitution and to imply that true democracy would produce a more equitable outcome." The Economic Freedom Front, led by Julius Malema, has been particularly vocal with this critique. How exactly this constitutional backlash will play out remains to be seen.

But apart from these macro-political differences, we see less of the kind of overt movement-countermovement interaction in South Africa than we did in the same-sex marriage case in the United States. The reason seems to have been that the logical place for countermovement activism to develop would have been the extremist wing of white nationalist mobilization, which was less concerned with issues of social constitutionalism than it was with their shattered dream of a White Republic. The National Party – the party of apartheid – had committed to and actively participated in the MPNP and CODESA I and II and sought to influence the resulting constitutional text, while those farther to the right, such as the (Afrikaner) Freedom Front, abstained from voting on the text. The Afrikaner Volksfront and the Freedom Front aimed to create a separate *Volkstaat* (an all-White Afrikaner enclave) and, earlier, disrupt the 1994 elections, rather than mount law-based mobilization against the constitution itself or the idea of social constitutionalism.

By looking to the case of social constitutionalism in South Africa, the significance of the four processes we identified in recent socio-legal and social movement scholarship – becomes evident. Social movements made constitutional change in South Africa possible. That constitutional change then presented activists with new opportunities for legal mobilization in the context of a new political/legal opportunity structure. Over time, continued legal mobilization resulted in the development of ideas about rights – that is, the social construction of the meaning of rights. This, in turn, created additional space for movements and countermovements to contest the contours of those rights. Examining these four processes together helps us to understand the relationship between law and social movements in the dramatic democratization of South Africa.

Conclusions

We began this essay with Derrick Bell's critique of the strategic choices of civil rights lawyers in pursuit of school integration in his article "Serving Two Masters?" Following the *Brown* decision and its aftermath, legal victories seemed to pile up, but Black families had raised concerns about the extent to which these victories would translate into real gains for their children. Ever since, debates regarding the viability of pursuing social change through the formal legal system have preoccupied both legal scholars and theorists of social movements. But for decades, these two strands of scholarship only dovetailed at their edges.

As we showed in Section 1, early social movement scholarship grew out of three traditions – collective behavior, neo-Marxism, and social history – none of which gave a central role to the law. Further, the methodological choices of social movement scholars – large-scale surveys, protest event analysis, and organizational analysis – dovetailed poorly with the case studies that were preferred by legal scholars.

In Section 2, we examined several strands of work that came out of the legal tradition: what came to be called "critical legal theory," which grew out of Bell's important critique of a legal strategy focused on rights; those working on "cause lawyering" in the tradition of Austin Sarat and Stuart Scheingold; and those whose work we grouped under the heading of "popular constitutionalism." Reaching from the 1970s to the end of the century and beyond, all three groups of scholars reached toward popular politics, but none of them drew directly on the advances being made in social movement scholarship.

This began to change in the 1990s. In Section 3, we tracked how legal and social movement scholarship began to converge following the debate between Gerald Rosenberg and Michael McCann. We found signs of this growing fusion in five areas: claims-making in the courts; making new laws and introducing new ways of interpreting existing law; shaping debates about the law within movements and the general public; the impact of courts on movements; and the enlightening turn to comparative studies. Together, these works provided us with a foundation for our own approach to blending the study of law and social movements.

In Section 4, we specified four key processes that seem to us to be most promising for affecting a fusion between these two scholarly traditions: legal mobilization, legal-political opportunity structure, social construction, and movement-countermovement interaction. In Section 5, we illustrated the work-ings and interactions of these processes from within our own work: the cam-paign for same-sex marriage in the United States and social constitutionalism in South Africa. We now turn to a broader question: How does the interaction of law and movements reflect deeper structural changes and conflicts at the base of capitalist society?

Inequality, Polarization, and Law and Movements

In our Introduction, we argued that the intersection of movements and the law is particularly pressing in an era of rising inequality and polarization. These factors have once again converged in America's current political and social conjuncture, as well as in many other countries across Europe and Latin America. As we saw in Section 4, the polarization in the party system and in the country made the abortion issue difficult to resolve within the nation's elective institutions, while growing inequality added fire to the divisions between right and left. A countermovement working both within and outside of America's institutions brought *Dobbs* to fruition in the Court, while an opposing movement based on race and social polarization leant support to the pro-abortion movement well beyond the courts.

We do not see a new civil war resulting from *Dobbs* and from the legislative progeny it produced in many state legislatures; nor do we see it arising from debate over the viability and utility of South Africa's commitment to social constitution, though current political struggles over rights and law present serious challenges for both the US and South Africa.[70] We only want to argue that in an era of growing inequality and paralyzing polarization, the courts have become a major fulcrum in the battle between opposing movements, even as access to justice for everyday people lags (Staszak 2015).

This is where one of our findings becomes glaringly obvious: that not only do movements affect the law but the courts in turn affect movement strategies and successes and their relation to the broader political system. The *Dobbs* decision in June 2023 lent force not only to Republican-heavy state legislatures to pass anti-abortion laws but gave the movement for women's choice the incentive to mobilize in the electoral arena. Similarly, the reliance of "lawfare" in South Africa, which was triggered, as Hugh Corder and Cora Hoexter (2017: 105) note, by "the rise of nepotism, corruption and state capture well as the abdication of governance responsibilities to the judiciary," has centered courts in just about all of the country's political struggles.[71]

Assuming that the "fused" research tradition is already well advanced, we want to raise a number of questions that we hope will help to guide its further development:

First, we wish to flag the importance of what we called "taking the comparative cure." This not only adds new cases to our methodological battery but will

---

[70] For an interim report on the effects of *Dobbs* on state-level legislation and litigation, see Masling et al. (2023).

[71] For more on lawfare in South Africa, see Le Roux and Davis (2019), Roux 2020, and Dent (2023).

also expand the range of scholarship with which American scholars engage. For example, some of the Latin American scholars whose work we examined have highlighted the "judicialization" of politics or the emergence of "lawfare," as South African scholars describe it. Given the growing attention to the courts in American politics after *Dobbs* and other Supreme Court decisions, we may be seeing a similar phenomenon of judicialization and lawfare in the United States.

Second, recent events in the United States – racial violence against Black Americans, the rollback of abortion rights, and the attempted undermining of democratic institutions, all phenomena that are by no means unique to the US context – offer a window into the utility of our approach. Efforts have been made to study the multiracial movement against white violence in the wake of the murder of young black boys and men by police officers in the late 2010s and the early 2020s. But to our knowledge, there have been no systematic efforts to relate these actions to the other major American movement of the last few years – white nationalism and its explosion in the insurrection at the Capitol on January 6th, 2021. Scholars may do well also to consider cross-national connections between the January 6th riot in the US and the January 2023 Brazilian ones. As the shocks of these explosions ebb, and scholarly efforts begin to take hold, what we have learned about movement-countermovement interaction may be applied to the co-occurrence of the movement for black lives and the rise of white nationalism, as well as nationalist right-wing movements around the world.

Third, from time to time in our essay, we noted the importance of what we called "cycles of contention." For example, in our account of the campaign in favor of same-sex marriage, we could not fail to note its extended scope – from the Hawaiian case that brought it to public notice to the back-and-forth of state-level referenda and court decisions, to the ultimate Supreme Court decisions that extended the right to marry to same-sex couples. But while tracing the movement-countermovement interaction that drove this process forward, we did not examine its extension into the "anti-woke" movement that emerged in a number of American states. Nor did we consider the push for sexual and reproductive rights in what has been called a "green wave" in Argentina, Colombia, Mexico, and Chile, or the countermobilization efforts already in the works in these countries.

In Section 5, we speculated that in the cycle of contention that led to the success of the same-sex marriage movement, gay and lesbian couples began to put pressure on LGBTQ advocacy groups, pushing them to put marriage equality higher on their agendas, after conservative forces began to win policy battles on the issue. But we ended that story with the Supreme Court's epochal decisions in *Windsor* and *Obergefall,* and did not pay sufficient attention to the possibility of the emergence of a new anti-libertarian movement at the grass-roots of American society. Those interested in same-sex marriage mobilization may be well-served to examine the cycle of contention at play in the United States, as well as struggle over same-sex marriage and gay rights as they play in such varied contexts as India (where the Supreme Court is currently hearing a case related to marriage equality) and Uganda (where the Parliament has just criminalized identifying as LGBTQ).[72] Extending attention to longer cycles of political/legal interactions before and after key legal disputes would invite scholars to "take the historical cure," as well as the comparative one.

In the wake of the Trump Presidency and his packing of the courts with his handpicked appointments, much attention has centered on the US Supreme Court. But largely missing from these debates has been the work of the lower levels of the legal system, which have haunted Trump's existence since he left office. For not only did over sixty lower court cases reject the former President's false electoral claims; prosecutors in New York State, New York City and Fulton County, Georgia, have not hesitated to take him on. As we write, New York City District Attorney Alvin Bragg has revived the investigation into Trump's paying off of porn star Stormy Daniels before he entered the White House in 2017 (Schonfeld 2023). That case is still evolving as we write, but the important point is that, faced by a former President and his allies who are threatening democracy, the lower levels of the judicial system have taken on its defense. Again, this phenomenon is not unique to the United States. As Verónica Michela and Kathryn Sikkink (2013) show, lower courts have been an active site for the pursuit of individual criminal accountability for human rights abuses, especially in Latin America through the use of private prosecutors (see also Michel 2018). We encourage scholars to further pursue the intersection of social movement mobilization, individual accountability, and the use of lower courts.

Finally, we have not given nearly enough attention to the structural conflicts that underlie both legal conflict and social movement mobilization around the world. The advances in both social movement and legal analysis often gesture toward these conflicts without tracing their impacts on current conflicts. We hope the next stage of social movement/legal scholarship will work at the junction between underlying structural conflicts and the relations between law and movements.

These are but some of the areas of un- or under-explored terrain that we hope the new generation of scholars who have been moving toward a fusion of social

---

[72] Scholars have also challenged the hyper-focus on marriage rights, identifying the importance of divorce rights, parenting rights, and other concerns that impact same-sex couples and families (see, e.g., Mayo-Adam 2023).

movement and socio-legal studies will take up. These scholars are increasingly interacting, learning from one another's findings, and promising – and this is our underlying hope – to complete the fusion that we have tried to advance in this essay. We cheer the progress they have already made and wish them luck in their endeavors.

References

Abel, Richard. 1995. *Politics by Other Means: Law in the Struggle against Apartheid, 1980–1994*. London: Routledge.

Ackerman, Bruce. 1991. *We the People: Foundations*. Cambridge, MA: Harvard University Press.

2000. *We the People: Transformations*. Cambridge, MA: Harvard University Press.

2018. *We the People: The Civil Rights Revolution*. Cambridge, MA: Harvard University Press.

2014. *The Civil Rights Revolution*. 1st ed. Cambridge, MA: Belknap Press: An Imprint of Harvard University Press.

Adam, Erin. (2017). "Intersectional Coalitions: The Paradoxes of Rights-Based Movement Building in LGBTQ and Immigrant Communities." *Law & Society Review* 51(1): 132–67.

African National Congress. 1994. "Strategy and Tactics." In *50th National Conference*. www.anc1912.org.za/50th-national-conference-strategy-and-tactics-of-the-african-national-congress/

Akbar, Amna A., Sameer M. Ashar, and Jocelyn Simonson. 2021. "Movement Law." *Stanford Law Review* 73: 821–84.

Albiston, Catherine R. 2005. "Bargaining in the Shadow of Social Institutions: Competing Discourses and Social Change in Workplace Mobilization of Civil Rights." *Law and Society Review* 39: 11–50.

Albiston, Catherine R., Scott L. Cummings, and Richard L. Abel. 2020. "Making Public Interest Lawyers in a Time of Crisis: An Evidence-Based Approach." *Georgetown Journal of Legal Ethics* 34: 227–87.

Alter, Karen J., and Jeanette Vargas. 2000. "Explaining Variation in the Use of European Litigation Strategies: European Community Law and British Gender Equality Policy." *Comparative Political Studies* 33(4): 452–82.

Alter, Karen J. 2014. *The New Terrain of International Law*. Princeton, NJ: Princeton University Press.

Alviar García, Helena, Karl Klare, and Lucy A. Williams, eds. 2016. *Social and Economic Rights in Theory and Practice: Critical Inquiries*. 1st ed. London: Routledge.

Aminzade, Ronald R., and Doug McAdam. 2001. "Emotions and Contentious Politics." In *Silence and Voice in the Study of Contentious Politics*, edited by Ronald R. Aminzade, Jack Goldstone, Doug McAdam, et al., Cambridge: Cambridge University Press, pp. 14–50.

Andersen, Ellen Ann. 2005. *Out of the Closets and Into the Courts: Legal Opportunity Structure and Gay Rights Litigation*. Ann Arbor: University of Michigan Press.

Andretta, Massimiliano, and Dontatella della Porta. 2014. "Surveying Protesters: Why and How." In *Methodological Practices in Social Movement Research*, edited by Donatella della Porta. Oxford: Oxford University Press.

Andrias, Kate, and Benjamin Sachs. 2020–21. "Constructing Countervailing Power: Law and Organizing in an Era of Political Inequality." *Yale Law Journal* 130: 546–777.

Arrington, Celeste L. 2019a. "Hiding in Plain Sight: Pseudonymity and Participation in Legal Mobilization." *Comparative Political Studies* 52(2): 310–41.

2019b. "The Mechanisms behind Litigation's 'Radiating Effects': Historical Grievances against Japan." *Law & Society Review* 53(1): 6–40.

Balkin, Jack M. 2011. *Constitutional Redemption: Political Faith in an Unjust World*. Cambridge, MA: Harvard University Press.

Balkin, Jack M., and Reva B. Siegel. 2006. "Principles, Practices, and Social Movements." *University of Pennsylvania Law Review* 154: 927–50.

Barkan, Steven E. 1980. "Political Trials and Resource Mobilization: Towards an Understanding of Social Movement Litigation." *Social Forces* 58: 944–61.

1984. "Legal Control of the Southern Civil Rights Movement." *American Sociological Review* 49: 552–65.

1985. *Protesters on Trial: Criminal Justice in the Southern Civil Rights and Vietnam Antiwar Movements*. New Brunswick, NJ: Rutgers University Press.

Barnes, Samuel, Max Kaase, Klaus R. Allerback, et al. 1979. *Political Action: Mass Participation in Five Western Democracies*. Thousand Oaks, CA: Sage.

Baum, Lawrence. 2008. *Judges and Their Audiences: A Perspective on Judicial Behavior*. 1 ed. Princeton, NJ: Princeton University Press.

Bell, Derrick A. Jr. 1976. "Serving Two Masters: Integration Ideals and Client Interests in School Desegregation Litigation." *Yale Law Journal* 85: 470–517.

Benford, Robert D., and David A. Snow. 2000. "Framing Processes and Social Movements: An Overview and Assessment." *Annual Review of Sociology* 26: 611–39.

Botero, Sandra, Daniel M. Brinks, and Ezequiel Gonzalez-Ocantos (Eds.). 2022. *The Limits of Judicialization: From Progress to Backlash in Latin America*. Cambridge: Cambridge University Press.

Boutcher, Steven A. 2010. "Mobilizing in the Shadow of the Law: Lesbian and Gay Rights in the Aftermath of *Bowers v Hardwick*." *Research in Social Movements, Conflict and Change* 31: 175–205.

2013. "Lawyering for Social Change: Pro Bono Publico, Cause Lawyering and the Social Movement Society." *Mobilization* 18: 179–96.

Boutcher, Steven A. and Holly J. McCammon. 2019. "Social Movements and Litigation." In *The Wiley-Blackwell Companion to Social Movements*, *2nd ed*, edited by David A. Snow, Sarah A. Soule, Hanspeter Kriesi, and Holly McCammon. London: Wiley-Blackwell, pp. 306–21.

Boutcher, Steven A., and James E. Stobaugh. 2013. "Law and Social Movements." In *Wiley-Blackwell Encyclopedia of Social and Political Movements*, edited by Donatella della Porta, Bert Klandermans, Doug McAdam, David Snow. New York: Blackwell, pp. 683–87.

Boutcher, Steven A., Corey Shdaimah, and Michael W. Yarbrough (Eds.). 2023. in preparation. *Research Handbook on Law, Movements, and Social Change*. Cheltenham: Elgar.

Brewer-Carías, Allan R. 2009. *Constitutional Protection of Human Rights in Latin America: A Comparative Study of Amparo Proceedings*. New York: Cambridge University Press.

Brinks, Daniel M., Varun Gauri, and Kyle Shen. 2015. "Social Rights Constitutionalism: Negotiating the Tension between the Universal and the Particular." *Annual Review of Law and Social Science* 11: 289–308.

Bunce, Valerie, and Wolchik, Sharon. 2011. *Defeating Authoritarian Leaders in Postcommunist Countries*. New York: Cambridge University Press.

Burstein, Paul. 1991. "Legal Mobilization as a Social Movement Tactic." *American Journal of Sociology* 96: 1201–25.

Canan, Penelope, and George W. Pring. 1988. "Studying Strategic Lawsuits against Public Participation: Mixing Quantitative and Qualitative Approaches." *Law and Society Review* 22: 385–95.

Chen, Alan. 2013. "Rights Lawyer Essentialism and the Next Generation of Rights Critics." *Michigan Law Review* 111: 903–29.

Chen, Alan K. and Scott L. Cummings. 2013. *Public Interest Lawyering: A Contemporary Perspective*. New York: Wolters Kluwer Law and Business.

Chua, Lynette J. 2014. *Mobilizing Gay Singapore: Rights and Resistance in an Authoritarian State*. Philadelphia: Temple University Press.

2018. *The Politics of Love in Myanmar: LGBT Mobilization and Human Rights as a Way of Life*. Stanford: Stanford University Press.

2019. "Legal Mobilization and Authoritarianism." *Annual Review of Law and Social Science* 15: 355–76.

Chua, Lynette, David Engel, and Sida Liu, eds. 2023. *The Asian Law and Society Reader*. Cambridge: Cambridge University Press.

Cichowski, Rachel A. 2007. *The European Court and Civil Society*. New York: Cambridge University Press.

Corder, Hugh, and Hoexter, Cora. 2017. "'Lawfare' in South Africa and Its Effects on the Judiciary." *African Journal of Legal Studies* 10(2–3): 105–26.

Coglianese, Gary. 2001. "Social Movements, Law, and Society: The Institutionalization of the Environmental Movement." *University of Pennsylvania Law Review* 150: 85–120.

Cole, David. 2012. "Where Liberty Lies: Civil Society and Individual Rights After 9/11." *Wayne State Law Review* 57: 1203–67.

2015. *Engines of Liberty*. New York: Basic Books.

Conant, Lisa J. 2002. *Justice Contained: Law and Politics in the European Union*. Ithaca, NY: Cornell University Press.

Couso, Javier, Alexandra Huneeus, and Rachel Sieder (Eds.). 2010. *Cultures of Legality: Judicialization and Political Activism in Latin America*. Cambridge: Cambridge University Press.

Crenshaw, Kimberlé Williams. 2011. "Twenty Years of Critical Race Theory: Looking Back to Move Forward." *Connecticut Law Review* 117: 1253–353.

Cummings, Scott L. 2016. "The Social Movement Turn in Law." *Law and Social Inquiry* 43: 360–416.

2017a. "Movement Lawyering." *U. of Illinois Law Review* 2117: 1646–732.

2017b. "The Puzzle of Social Movements in American Legal Theory." *UCLA Law Review* 64: 1552–658.

2018a. *Blue and Green: The Drive for Justice in America's Port*. Cambridge, MA: MIT Press.

2018b. "Law and Social Movements: Reimagining the Progressive Canon." *Wisconsin Law Review* 3: 441–501.

2024. "Lawyers in Backsliding Democracy." *California Law Review* 112: 1–52.

Cummings, Scott L., and Douglas NeJaime. 2010. "Lawyering for Marriage Equality." *UCLA Law Review* 57: 1235–331.

Davis, Gerald F., Doug McAdam, W. Richard Scott, and Mayer N. Zald, eds. 2005. *Social Movements and Organization Theory*. New York: Cambridge University Press.

de Fazio, Gianluca. 2012. "Legal Opportunity Structure and Social Movement Strategy in Northern Ireland and Southern United States." *International Journal of Contemporary Sociology* 53: 3–22.

Delgado, Richard, and Jean Stefano. 2001. *Critical Race Theory: An Introduction*. New York: New York University Press.

della Porta, Donatella. 2014a. "Surveying Protesters: Why and How." In *Methodological Practices in Social Movement Research*, edited by D. Della Porta. Oxford: Oxford University Press, pp. 308–34.

(Ed.). 2014b. *Methodological Practices in Social Movement Research*. Oxford: Oxford University Press.

della Porta, Donatella and Mario Diani. 2006. *Social Movements: An Introduction, 2nd ed.* Malden: Blackwell's.

Dent, Kate. 2023. *Lawfare and Judicial Legitimacy: The Judicialisation of Politics in the Case of South Africa.* London: Routledge.

Dickinson, John 1985. "Letters from an American Farmer." In *The Writings of John Dickinson. Political Writings 1764–1774*, edited by Paul Leicester Ford. Philadelphia: Historical Society of Pennsylvania, pp. 312–25.

Dorf, Michael C., and Michael S. Chu. 2018. "Lawyers as Activists: From the Airport to the Courtroom." In *The Resistance: The Dawn of the Anti-Trump Opposition Movement*, edited by David S. Meyer and Sidney Tarrow. New York: Oxford University Press, pp. 127–42.

Dorf, Michael C., and Sidney Tarrow. 2014. "Strange Bedfellows: How an Anticipatory Countermovement Brought Same-Sex Marriage into the Public Arena." *Law and Social Inquiry* 39: 449–73.

Dugan, Kimberly B. 2004. "Strategy and 'Spin': Opposing Movement Frames in an Anti-Gay Voter Initiative." *Sociological Focus* 37(3): 213–33.

Dugard, Jackie. 2006. "'Court of First Instance?' Towards a Pro-poor Jurisdiction for the South African Constitutional Court." *South African Journal on Human Rights* 22: 261–82.

2015. "Closing the Doors of Justice: An Examination of the Constitutional Court's Approach to Direct Access, 1995–2013." *South African Journal on Human Rights* 31: 112–35.

Dugard, John. 1990. "Toward Racial Justice in South Africa." In *Constitutionalism and Rights: The Influence of the United States Constitution Abroad*, edited by Louis Henken and Albert Rosenthal. New York: Columbia University Press, pp. 349–80.

2015. *Human Rights and the South African Legal Order.* Princeton: Princeton University Press.

Edelman, Lauren B., Gwendolyn Leachman, and Doug McAdam. 2010. "On Law, Organizations, and Social Movements." *Annual Review of Law and Social Science* 6: 683–85.

Elkins, Zachary, and Tom Ginsburg. 2021. "Characteristics of National Constitutions Version 3.0." In *Comparative Constitutions Project.* comparativeconstitutionsproject.org.

Engel, David M., and Jaruwan S. Engel. 2010. *Tort, Custom, and Karma: Globalization and Legal Consciousness in Thailand.* Stanford: Stanford Law Books.

Epp, Charles R. 1998. *The Rights Revolution: Lawyers, Activists and Supreme Courts in Comparative Perspective.* Chicago: University of Chicago Press.

2009. *Making Rights Real: Activists, Bureaucrats, and the Creation of the Legalistic State*. Chicago: University of Chicago Press.

Eskridge, William N. Jr. 2001. "Channeling: Identity-Based Social Movements and Public Law." *U. Penn. Law Rev.* 150: 419–525.

Eskridge, William N. Jr., and Gary R. Spedale. 2007. *Gay Marriage: For Better or for Worse? What We've Learned from the Evidence*. New York: Oxford University Press.

Evans Case, Rhonda, and Terri E. Givens. 2010. "Re-Engineering Legal Opportunity Structures in the European Union." *Journal of Common Market Studies* 48: 221–41.

Ewick, Patricia and Susan S. Silbey. 1998. *The Common Place of Law: Stories from Everyday Life*. Chicago: University of Chicago Press.

Faux, Marian. 1988. *Roe Versus Wade: The Untold Story of the Landmark Supreme Court Decision That Made Abortion Legal*. New York: Scribner.

Fetner, Tina. 2008. *How the Religious Right Shaped Lesbian and Gay Activism*. Minneapolis: University of Minnesota Press.

Fineman, Martha A. 1992. "Feminist Theory in Law: The Difference It Makes." *Columbia Journal of Gender and Law* 2: 1–23.

Fisher, Dana R. 2019. *American Resistance: From the Women's March to the Blue Wave*. New York: Columbia University Press.

Fisk, Catherine L., and Diana S. Reddy. 2020. "Protection by Law, Repression by Law: Bringing Labor Back into the Study of Law and Social Movements." *Emory Law Journal* 70: 62–152.

Fowkes, James. 2016. *Building the Constitution: The Practice of Constitutional Interpretation in Post-Apartheid South Africa*. Cambridge: Cambridge University Press.

Galanter, Marc. 1974. "Why the 'Haves' Come Out Ahead: Speculations on the Limits of Legal Change." *Law and Society Review* 9: 95–160.

Gallagher, Janice. 2022. *Bootstrap Justice: The Search for Mexico's Disappeared*. New York: Oxford University Press.

Gallagher, Mary. 2006. "Mobilizing the Law in China: 'Informed Disenchantment' and the Development of Legal Consciousness." *Law and Society Review* 4: 783–816.

2017. *Authoritarian Legality in China: Law, Workers and the State*. New York and Cambridge: Cambridge University Press.

Gallagher, Mary, and Yujeong Yang. 2017. "Getting Schooled: Legal Mobilization as an Educative Process." *Law and Social Inquiry* 42: 163–93.

Gamson, William A., and David S. Meyer. 1996. "Framing Political Opportunity." In *Comparative Perspectives on Social Movements: Political Opportunities, Mobilizing Structures, and Cultural Framings*, edited by Doug McAdam,

John McCarthy, and Mayer N. Zald. Cambridge: Cambridge University Press, pp. 275–90.

Glendon, Mary Ann. 1991. *Rights Talk: The Impoverishment of Political Discourse*. New York: The Free Press.

Goffman, Erving. 1974. *Frame Analysis: An Essay on the Organization of Experience*. New York: Harper Colophon.

Goldstone, Jack A., and Charles Tilly. 2001. "Threat (and Opportunity): Popular Action and State Response in the Dynamics of Contentious Action." In *Silence and Voice in the Study of Contentious Politics*, edited by Ronald Aminzade. New York: Cambridge University Press.

González Ocantos, Ezequiel. 2014. "Persuade Them or Oust Them: Crafting Judicial Change and Transitional Justice in Argentina." *Comparative Politics* 46: 479–98.

  2016. *Shifting legal Visions: Judicial Change and Human Rights Trials in Latin America*. New York: Cambridge University Press.

Goodwin, Jeff, James M. Jasper, and Francesca Polletta eds. 2001. *Passionate Politics: Emotions and Social Movements*. Chicago: University of Chicago Press.

Guinier, Lani. 2009. "Courting the People: Demosprudence and the Law/ Politics Divide." *Boston University Law Review* 89: 539–61.

Guinier, Lani, and Gerald Torres. 2014. "Changing the Wind: Notes towards a Demosprudence of Law and Social Movements." *Yale Law Journal* 123: 2740–804.

Handler, Joel F. 1978. *Social Movements and the Legal System*. New York: Academic Press.

Haney-López, Ian. 1997. *White by Law: The Legal Construction of Race*. New York: New York University Press.

Harris, Mark L. 2004. "Civil Society in Post-Revolutionary America." In *Empire and Nation: The American Revolution in the Atlantic World*, edited by Eliga H. Gould and Peter S. Onuf. Baltimore, MD: Johns Hopkins University Press.

Hendley, Kathryn. 1999. "Rewriting the Rules of the Game in Russia: The Neglected Issue of Demand for Law." *East European Constitutional Review* 8(4): 89–95.

Hilson, Chris. 2002. "New Social Movements: The Role of Legal Opportunity." *Journal of European Public Policy* 9: 238–55.

  2013. "The Courts and Social Movements: Two Literatures and Two Methodologies." *Mobilizing Ideas*: 1–3. https://mobilizingideas.wordpress .com/2013/02/18/the-courts-and-social-movements-two-literatures-and-two-methodologies/.

2016. "Environmental SLAPPS in the UK: Threat or Opportunity?" *Environmental Politics* 25: 248–67.

Hollis-Brusky, Amanda I. 2015. *Ideas with Consequences: The Federalist Society and the Conservative Counterrevolution*. New York: Oxford University Press.

Horwitz, Morton. 1992. *The Transformation of American Law, 1870–1960*. New York: Oxford University Press.

Hunter, Nan D. 2017. "Varieties of Constitutional Experience: Democracy and the Marriage Equality Campaign". *UCLA Law Review* 64: 1662–726.

Hutter, Sven. 2014. "Protest Event Analysis and Its Offspring." In *Methodological Practices in Social Movement Research*, edited by Donatella della Porta. Oxford: Oxford University Press.

Jenkins, J. Craig, and Charles Perrow. 1977. "Insurgency of the Powerless: Farm Worker Movements (1946–1972)." *American Sociological Review* 42: 249–68.

Johnson, Ben, and Logan Strother. 2021. "The Supreme Court's (Surprising?) Indifference to Public Opinion." *Political Research Quarterly* 74: 18–34.

Kahraman, Filiz. 2018. "A New Era for Labor Activism? Strategic Mobilization of Human Rights against Blacklisting." *Law and Social Inquiry* 43: 1279–307.

Kalman, Laura. 1998. *The Strange Career of Legal Liberalism*. New Haven: Yale University Press.

Keck, Margaret, and Kathryn Sikkink. 1998. *Activists beyond Borders: Transnational Activist Networks in International Politics*. Ithaca: Cornell University Press.

Keck, Thomas M. 2009. "Beyond Backlash: Assessing the Impact of Judicial Decisions on LGBT Rights." *Law and Society Review* 43: 151–85.

Kelemen, R. Daniel. 2011. *Eurolegalism: The Transformation of Law and Regulation in the European Union*. Cambridge, MA: Harvard University Press.

Keniston, Kenneth. 1960. *Young Radicals: Notes on Committed Youth*. New York: Harcourt, Brace.

Kennedy, Duncan. 2006. *The Rise and Fall of Classical Legal Thought*. Washington, DC: Beard Books.

Kim, Claudia Junghyun, and Celeste L. Arrington. 2023. "Knowledge Production through Legal Mobilization: Environmental Activism against the U.S. Military Bases in East Asia." *Law & Society Review* 57(2): 162–88.

Kim, Jieun, Rachel E. Stern, Benjamin L. Liebman, and Xiaohan Wu. 2021. "Closing Open Government: Grassroots Policy Conversion of China's Open government Information Regulation and its Aftermath." *Comparative Political Studies* 55: 318–32.

Klandermans, Bert, and Nonna Mayer. 2006. *Extreme Right Activists in Europe: Through the Magnifying Glass*. London: Routledge.

Klare, Karl. 1978. "Law-Making as Praxis." *Telos* 40: 123–35.

1978–9. "Judicial Deradicalization of the Wagner Act and the Origins of Modern Legal Consciousness, 1937–1941." *Minnesota Law Review* 62: 265–339.

Klarman, Michael J. 2004. *From Jim Crow to Civil Rights: The Supreme Court and the Struggle for Racial Equality*. New York: Oxford University Press.

2013. *From the Closet to the Altar: Courts, Backlash, and the Struggle for Same-Sex Marriage*. New York: Oxford University Press.

2020. "The Degradation of American Democracy – and the Court." *Harvard Law Review* 134: 4–62.

Klug, Heinz. 2000. *Constituting Democracy: Law, Globalism and South Africa's Political Reconstruction*. Cambridge: Cambridge University Press.

2016. "Challenging Constitutionalism in Post-Apartheid South Africa." *Constitutional Studies* 2: 41–58.

Kramer, Larry D. 2001. "Forward: We the Court." *Harvard Law Review* 115: 4–169.

2004. *The People Themselves: Popular Constitutionalism and Judicial Review*. New York: Oxford University Press.

Kriesi, Hanspeter, Ruud Koopmans, Jan Willem Duyvendak, and Marco Giugni. 1995. *New Social Movements in Western Europe: A Comparative Analysis*. Minneapolis: University of Minnesota Press.

Le Roux, Michelle, and Dennis Davis. 2019. *Lawfare: Judging Politics in South Africa*. Johannesburg: Jonathan Ball.

Lehoucq, Emilio, and Whitney K. Taylor. 2019. "Conceptualizing Legal Mobilization: How Should We Understand the Deployment of Legal Strategies." *Law and Social Inquiry* 45: 166–93. www.cambridge.org/ core/journals/law-and-social-inquiry/article/abs/conceptualizing-legal-mobilization-how-should-we-understand-the-deployment-of-legal-strat egies/A73F0A497C59751DE7E9606F1372F827.

Lemaitre, Julieta and Rachel Sieder. 2017. "The Moderating Influence of International Courts on Social Movements." *Health and Human Rights* 19: 149–60.

Levinson, Sanford. 2014. "Popular Sovereignty and the United States Constitution: Tensions in the Ackermanian Program." *Yale Law Journal* 123: 2644–74.

Levit, Nancy and Robert M. Verchick. 2016. *Feminist Legal Theory: A Primer*. New York: NYU Press.

Liu, Sida and Terence C. Halliday. 2016. *Criminal Defense in China: The Politics of Lawyers at Work*. Cambridge: Cambridge University Press.

Lobel, Orly. 2007. "The Paradox of Extralegal Activism: Critical Legal Consciousness and Transformative Politics." *Harvard Law Review* 120: 937–88.

Lodge, Tom. 1983. *Black Politics in South Africa Since 1945*. New York: Addison Wesley Longmans.

Lovell, George. 2012. *This Is Not Civil Rights: Discovering Rights Talk in 1939 America*. Chicago: University of Chicago Press.

Mahoney, James. 2000. "Path Dependence in Historical Sociology." *Theory and Society* 24: 507–48.

Mandela, Nelson. 1995. *Long Walk to Freedom: The Autobiography of Nelson Mandela*. Boston: Back Bay Books.

Mansbridge, Jane. 1986. *Why We Lost the ERA*. Chicago: University of Chicago Press.

Margulies, Joseph. 2013. *What Changed When Everything Changed: 9/11 and the Making of National Identity*. New Haven: Yale University Press.

Margulies, Joseph and M. Metcalf. 2011. "Terrorizing Academia." *Journal of Legal Education* 60: 433–71.

Marks, Gary and Doug McAdam. 1996. "Social Movements and the Changing Structure of Political Opportunity in the European Union." In *Governance in the European Union*, edited by Gary Marks, Fritz W. Scharpf, Philippe C. Schmitter, Wolfgang Streeck. Thousand Oaks, CA: Sage, pp. 95–120.

Marshall, Anna-Maria. 2003. "Injustice Frames, Legality, and the Everyday Construction of Sexual Harassment." *Law and Social Inquiry* 28: 659–89.

Mayo-Adam, Erin. 2023 "Marriage Equality's Wasteland: On the Struggle for Queer Reproductive Justice." Paper Presented at the 2023 Law & Society Association Annual Meeting.

McAdam, Doug. 1982[1999]. *Political Process and the Development of Black Insurgency, 1930–1970*. Chicago: University of Chicago Press.

McAdam, D., and S. Tarrow. 2019. "Strands of Classical Sociological Theory in the Study of Social Movements." In *The Handbook of Classical Sociological Theory*, edited by Seth Abrutyn and Omar Lizardo. Switzerland: Springer, pp. 467–85.

McAdam, Doug, Sidney Tarrow, and Charles Tilly. 2001. *Dynamics of Contention*. New York: Cambridge University Press.

McCammon, Holly J. 2012. *The U.S. Women's Jury Movements and Strategic Adaptation: A More Just Verdict*. New York: Cambridge University Press.

McCann, Michael W. 1992. "The Hollow Hope: Can Courts Bring About Social Change? by Gerald N. Rosenberg." *Law and Social Inquiry* 17: 715–43.

1994. *Rights at Work: Pay Equity Reform and the Politics of Legal Mobilization*. Chicago: University of Chicago Press.

1996. "Causal versus Constitutive Explanations (or, On the Difficult of Being So Positive)." *Law and Social Inquiry* 21: 457–82.

(Ed.). 2006. *Law and Social Movements*. Burlington, VT: Ashgate.

McCann, Michael, and Filiz Kahraman. 2021. "On the Interdependence of Liberal and Illiberal/Authoritarian Legal Forms in Racial Capitalist Regimes ... The Case of the United States." *Annual Review of Law and Social Science* 17(1): 483–503.

McCann, Michael W., and George I. Lovell. 2020. *Union By Law: Filipino American Labor Activists, Rights Radicalism, and Racial Capitalism*. Chicago: University of Chicago Press.

McCann, Michael W., and William Hortom. 2004. *Distorting the Law: Politics, Media, and the Litigation Crisis*. Chicago: University of Chicago Press.

McCarthy, John, and Mayer N. Zald. 1973. *The Trend of Social Movements in America: Professionalization and Resource Mobilization*. Morristown: General Learning Press.

1977. "Resource Mobilization and Social Movements: A Partial Theory." *American Journal of Sociology* 82: 1212–41.

McCarthy, John, Clark McPhail, and Jackie Smith. 1996. "Images of Protest: Estimating Selection Bias in Media Coverage of Washington Demonstrations." *American Sociological Review* 61: 478–99.

Meierhenrich, Jens. 2008. *The Legacies of Law: Long-run Consequences of Legal Development in South Africa, 1652–2000*. Cambridge: Cambridge University Press.

Merry, Sally Engle. 1990. *Getting Justice and Getting Even: Legal Consciousness among Working-Class Americans*. Chicago: University of Chicago Press.

2006a. "Transnational Human Rights and Local Activism: Mapping the Middle." *American Anthropologist* 108: 38–51.

2006b. *Human Rights and Gender Violence: Translating International Law into Local Justice*. Chicago: University of Chicago Press.

Meyer, David S., and Steven A. Boutcher. 2008. "Signals and Spillover: Brown V. Board of Education and Other Social Movements." *Perspectives on Politics* 5: 81–93.

Meyer, David S., and Suzanne Staggenborg. 1996. "Movements, Countermovements, and the Structure of Political Opportunity." *American Journal of Sociology* 101: 1628–60.

1998. "Countermovement Dynamics in Federal Systems: A Comparison of Abortion Politics in Canada and the United States." *Research in Political Sociology* 8: 209–40.

2022. "Understanding Countermovements." In *Handbook of Anti-Environmentalism*, edited by David Tindall, Mark C. J. Stoddard, and Dunlap Riley E. Cheltenham: Edward Elgar, pp. 23–42.

Michel, Verónica. 2018. *Prosecutorial Accountability and Victim's Rights in Latin America*. New York: Cambridge University Press.

Michel, Verónica, and Kathryn Sikkink. 2013. "Human Rights Prosecutions and the Participation Rights of Victims in Latin America." *Law and Society Review* 47: 873–907.

Mottl, Tahi. 1980. "The Analysis of Countermovements." *Social Problems* 27: 620–35.

Moustafa, Tamir. 2014. "Law and Courts in Authoritarian Regimes." *Annual Review of Law and Social Science* 10: 281–99.

Murphy, Hannah, and Aynsley Kellow. 2013. "Forum Shopping in Global Governance: Understanding States, Business and NGOs in Multiple Arenas." *Global Policy* 4(2): 139–49.

NeJaime, Douglas. 2011. "Winning Through Losing." *Iowa Law Review* 96: 943–1012.

2012. "The Legal Mobilization Dilemma." *Emory Law Journal* 61: 664–733.

Nonet, Philippe, and Philip Selznick. 2001. *Law and Society in Transition*. New Brunswick, NJ: Transaction.

Offe, Claus. 1985. "New Social Movements: Challenging the Boundaries of Institutional Politics." *Social Research* 52: 817–68.

Olson, Mancur. 1965. *The Logic of Collective Action*. Cambridge, MA: Harvard University Press.

Olson, Susan M. 1984. *Clients and Lawyers: Securing the Rights of Disabled Persons*. Westport: Greenwood Press.

Paris, Michael. 2009. *Framing Political Opportunity: Law and the Politics of School Finance Reform*. Stanford: Stanford University Press.

Parker, Christopher S., and Matt A. Barreto. 2013. *Change They Can't Believe In: The Tea Party and Reactionary Politics in America*. Princeton: Princeton University Press.

Pavone, Tommaso. 2022. *The Ghostwriters: Lawyers and the Politics behind the Judicial Construction of Europe*. Cambridge: Cambridge University Press.

Perley Masling, Sharon, Saghi Fattahian, and Jonathan Zimmerman. 2023. "Evolving Laws and Litigation Post-Dobbs. The State of Reproductive Rights as of January 2023." www.morganlewis.com/pubs/2023/01/evolving-laws-and-litigation-post-dobbs-the-state-of-reproductive-rights-as-of-january-2023.

Phillips, Laura. 2017. "History of South Africa's Bantustans." *Oxford Research Encyclopedia of African History* (July). https://doi.org/10.1093/acrefore/9780190277734.013.80.

Piven, Frances Fox and Richard Cloward. 1992. "The Normalization of Collective Protest." In *Frontiers in Social Movement Theory*, edited by Aldon Morris and Carol McClurg Mueller. New Haven: Yale University Press, pp. 301–25.

Polletta, Francesca. 2000. "The Structural Context of Novel Rights Claims: Southern Civil Rights Organizing, 1961-1966." *Law and Society Review* 34: 367–406.

Post, Robert. 2006. "Originalism as a Political Practice: The Right's Living Constitution." *Fordham Law Review* 75: 545–74.

Post, Robert, and Reva B. Siegel. 2007. "Roe Rage: Democratic Constitutionalism and Backlash." *Harvard Civil Rights and Civil Liberties Law Review* 42: 373–434.

Prabhat, Devyani. 2016. *Unleashing the Force of Law: Legal Mobilization, National Security, and Basic Freedoms*. London: Palgrave Macmillan.

Pring, George W. 1989. "SLAPPS: Strategic Lawsuits against Public Participation." *Pace Environmental Law Review* 7: 3–21.

Randeria, Shalini. 2007. "Legal Pluralism, Social Movements and the Post-Colonial State in India: Fractured Sovereignty and Differential Citizenship Rights." In *Another Knowledge Is Possible: Beyond Northern Epistemologies*, edited by Bonaventura de Sousa Santos. London: Verso, pp. 41–75.

Rosenberg, Gerald N. 1991. *The Hollow Hope: Can Courts Bring About Social Change?* Chicago: University of Chicago.

1996. "Positivism, Interpretivism, and the Study of Law." *Law and Social Inquiry* 2(1): 435–55.

2022. "Abortion After Dobbs." *Law and Courts Newsletter* 32: 18–41.

2023. *The Hollow Hope: Can Courts Bring About Social Change?* Chicago: University of Chicago Press.

Roux, Theunis. 2020. "The Constitutional Court's 2018 Term: Lawfare or Window on the Struggle for Democratic Social Transformation." *Constitutional Court Review* 10: 1–42.

Rucht, Dieter. 1998. "The Structure and Culture of Collective Protest in Germany since 1950." In *The Social Movement Society: Contentious Politics for a New Century*, edited by David Meyer and Sidney Tarrow. Boulder: Rowman and Littlefield, pp. 29–57.

Ruibal, Alba. 2023. "Legal Mobilization: Social Movements and the Judicial System across Latin America." In *Oxford Handbook of Latin American*

Social Movements, edited by Federico Rossi. Oxford: Oxford University Press, pp. 746–60.

Sarat, Austin (Ed.). 2021. *The Legacy of Stuart Scheingold*. Bingley: Emerald Group.

Sarat, Austin and Stuart A. Scheingold (Eds.). 1997. *Cause Lawyering: Political Commitments and Professional Responsibilities*. Oxford: Oxford University Press.

2001. *Cause Lawyering and the State in the Global Era*. Oxford: Oxford University Press.

2005. *The Worlds Cause Lawyers Make*. Stanford: Stanford University Press.

2006. *Cause Lawyers and Social Movements*. Stanford: Stanford University Press.

2008. *The Cultural Lives of Cause Lawyers*. Stanford: Stanford University Press.

Scheingold, Stuart A. 1974. *The Politics of Rights: Lawyers, Public Policy, and Political Change*. Stanford: Stanford University Press.

Scheingold, Stuart A., and Austin Sarat. 2004. *Something to Believe in: Politics, Professionalism, and Cause Lawyering*. Stanford: Stanford University Press.

Schlozman, Daniel. 2015. *When Movements Anchor Parties: Electoral Alignments in American History*. Princeton: Princeton University Press.

Schonfeld, Zach. 2023. "Prospects Rise for NY Charges against Trump in Stormy Daniels Case." *Yahoo News*. https://news.yahoo.com/prospects-rise-ny-charges-against-110000454.html2023.

Scott, James C. 1985. *Weapons of the Weak: Everyday forms of Resistance*. New Haven: Yale University Press.

1990. *Domination and the Arts of Resistance: Hidden Transcripts*. New Haven: Yale University Press.

Sidel, Mark. 2004. *More Secure, Less Free? Antiterrorism Policy and Civil Liberties after September 11*. Ann Arbor: University of Michigan Press.

Sieder, Rachel, Line Schjolden, and Alan Angell (Eds.). 2005. *The Judicialization of Politics in Latin America*. New York: Basingstoke.

Siegel, Reva B. 2001. "Text in Context: Gender and the Constitution from a Social Movement Perspective." *University of Pennsylvania Law Review* 150. 297 351

2002. "She the People: The Nineteenth Amendment, Sex Equality, Federalism and the Family." *Harvard Law Review* 113: 1–94.

2008. "Dead or Alive: Originalism as Popular Constitutionalism in Heller." *Harvard Law Review* 122: 191–245.

2023. "Memory Games: Dobbs's Originalism as Anti-Democratic Living Constitutionalism—and Some Pathways for Resistance." *Texas Law Review* 101: 1–78.

Sikkink, Kathryn. 2011. *The Justice Cascade: How Human Rights Prosecutions Are Changing World Politics*. 1 ed. New York: W. W. Norton & Company.

Sikkink, Kathryn. 2016. *The Justice Cascade: How Human Rights Prosecutions are Changing World Politics*. New York: W.W. Norton.

Silverstein, Helena. 1996. *Unleashing Rights: Law, Meaning, and the Animal Rights Movement*. Ann Arbor: University of Michigan Press.

Simmons, Erica. 2016. *Meaningful Resistance*. New York: Cambridge University Press.

Skowronek, Steven. 1997. *The Politics Presidents Make: Leadership from John Adams to Bill Clinton*. Cambridge, MA: Harvard University Press.

Smith, David. 2021. "How Did Republicans Turn Critical Race Theory into a Winning Electoral Issue?" *The Guardian*. www.theguardian.com/us-news/2021/nov/03/republicans-critical-race-theory-winning-electoral-issue. 2021.

Snow, David A., E. Burke Rochford, Jr., Steven K. Worden, and Robert D. Benford. 1986. "Frame Alignment Processes, Micromobilization and Movement Participation." *American Sociological Review* 51: 464–81.

Soley, Ximena. 2019. "The Crucial Role of Human Rights NGOs in the Inter-American System." *American Journal of International Law* 113: 355–9.

Spade, Dean, and Craig Willse. 2015. *Marriage Will Never Set Us Free*. Melbourne: Subversion Press.

Sparks, Allister. 1996. *Tomorrow is Another Country: The Inside Story of South Africa's Road to Change*. Chicago: University of Chicago Press.

Staggenborg, Suzanne. 1991. *The Pro-Choice Movement: Organization and Activism in the Abortion Conflict*. New York: Oxford University Press.

1995. "The Survival of the Pro-Choice Movement." *Journal of Policy History* 7: 160–76.

Staszak, Sarah L. 2015. *No Day in Court: Access to Justice and the Politics of Judicial Retrenchment*. New York: Oxford University Press.

Stern, Rachel E. 2013. *Environmental Litigation in China: A Study in Political Ambivalence*. Cambridge: Cambridge University Press.

Stone, Amy. 2012. *Gay Rights at the Ballot Box*. Minneapolis: University of Minnesota Press.

Szymanski, Anne-Marie E. 2003. *Pathways to Prohibition: Radicals, Moderates, and Social Movement Outcomes*. Durham: Duke University Press.

Tam, Waikeung. 2013. *Legal Mobilization under Authoritarianism: The Case of Post-Colonial Hong Kong*. Cambridge: Cambridge University Press.

Tarrow, Sidney. 1989. *Democracy and Disorder: Protest and Politics in Italy, 1965-1974*. Oxford: Oxford University Press.

1996. "States and Opportunities: The Political Structuring of Social Movements." In *Comparative Perspectives on Social Movements: Political Opportunities, Mobilizing Structures, and Cultural Framings*, edited by McAdam Doug, John D. McCarthy, and Mayer N. Zald. Cambridge: Cambridge University Press, pp. 62–92.

2011. *Power in Movement: Social Movements and Contentious Politics*. 3rd ed. Cambridge: Cambridge University Press.

2012. *Strangers at the Gates: Movements and States in Contentious Politics*. Cambridge: Cambridge University Press.

2021. *Movements and Parties: Critical Connections in American Political Development*. New York: Cambridge University Press.

2022 [1994, 2011]. *Power in Movement: Social Movements and Contentious Politics*. New York: Cambridge University Press.

Taylor, Verta, Nella Van Dyke, Katrina Kimport, and Ellen Ann Andersen. 2009. "Culture and Mobilization: Tactical Repertoires, Same-Sex Weddings, and the Impact on Gay Activism." *American Sociological Review* 74: 865–86.

Taylor, Whitney K. 2018. "Ambivalent Legal Mobilization: Perceptions of Justice and the Use of the Tutela in Colombia." *Law and Society Review* 52: 337–67.

2020. "On the Social Construction of Legal Grievances: Evidence from Colombia and South Africa." *Comparative Political Studies* 53: 1326–56.

2023a. "Judicial Agency and the Adjudication of Social Rights." *Human Rights Quarterly* 45: 283–309.

2023b. *The Social Constitution: Embedding Social Rights in Colombia*. New York: Cambridge University Press.

Teles, Steven M. 2008. *Rise of the Conservative Legal Movement*. Princeton: Princeton University Press.

Tezcür, Güneş Murat. 2009. "Judicial Activism in Perilous Times: The Turkish Case." *Law & Society Review* 43(2): 305–36.

Thiele, Leslie Paul. 1993. "Making Democracy Safe for the World: Social Movements and Global Politics." *Alternatives: Global, Local, Political* 18(3): 273–305.

Tilly, Charles. 1979. *From Mobilization to Revolution*. Reading: Addison-Wesley.

1995. *Popular Contention in Great Britain, 1758-1834*. Cambridge, MA. Harvard University Press.

Trochev, Alexei. 2008. *Judging Russia: The Role of the Constitutional Court in Russian Politics 1990–2006*. New York: Cambridge University Press.

Trowbridge, David 2022. "Beyond Litigation." *Law and Society Review* 56: 286–308.

Tushnet, Mark. 1991. "Critical Legal Studies: A Political History." *Yale Law Journal* 100: 1515–44.

Unger, Robert. 1983. *The Critical Legal Studies Movement.* Cambridge, MA: Harvard University Press.

Van Cott, Donna Lee. 2000. *The Friendly Liquidation of the Past: The Politics of Diversity in Latin America.* Pittsburgh: University of Pittsburgh Press.

2005. *From Movements to Parties in Latin America: The Evolution of Ethnic Politics.* Cambridge: Cambridge University Press.

Vanhala, Lisa. 2010. *Making Rights a Reality? Disability Rights Activists and Legal Mobilization.* Cambridge: Cambridge University Press.

2011. "Legal Mobilization." In *Oxford Bibliographies.* www.oxfordbibliogra phies.com/display/document/obo-9780199756223/obo-9780199756223-0031.xml.

2012. "Legal Opportunity Structures and the Paradox of Legal Mobilization by the Environmental Movement in the UK." *Law and Society Review* 46: 523–56.

2018. "Shaping the Structure of Legal Opportunities: Environmental NGOs Bringing International Environmental Procedural Rights Back Home." *Law and Policy* 40: 110–27.

2022. "Environmental Legal Mobilization." *Annual Review of Law and Social Science* 18: 101–17.

Vüllers, Johannes, and Sebastian Hellmeier. 2022. "Does Counter-Mobilization Contain Right-Wing Populist Movements? Evidence from Germany." *European Journal of Political Research* 61: 21–45.

West, Robin. 2018. "Women in the Legal Academy: A Brief History of Feminist Legal Theory." *Fordham Law Review* 87: 977–1003.

Wilson, Bruce. 2009. "Institutional Reform and Rights Revolution in Latin America: The Cases of Costa Rica and Colombia." *Journal of Politics in Latin America* 1: 59–85.

Wilson, Bruce, and Camilla Gianella-Malca. 2019. "Overcoming the Limits of Legal Opportunity Structures: LGBT Rights' Divergent Paths in Costa Rica and Colombia." *Latin American Politics and Society* 61: 138–63.

Wilson, Bruce, and Juan Carlos Rodriguez Cordero. 2006. "Legal Opportunity Structures and Social Movements: The Effects of Institutional Change on Costa Rican Politics." *Comparative Political Studies* 39(3): 325–51.

Zald, Mayer N., and John McCarthy (Eds.). 1987. *Social Movements in an Organizational Society: Collected Essays*. New Brunswick: Transaction Books.

Zemans, Frances Kahn. 1983. "The Neglected Role of the Law in the Political System." *American Political Science Review* 77: 690–703.

Acknowledgments

This Element has profited from helpful advice from Erin Mayo-Adam, Celeste Arrington, Scott Cummings, Michael Dorf, Jerry Goldberg, Chris Hilson, Karl Klare, Michael Klarman, Joseph Margulies, Doug McAdam, Michael McCann, David S. Meyer, Douglas NeJaime, Aziz Rana, Gerry Rosenberg, Steve Schiffrin, Reva Siegel, Suzanne Staggenborg, and two anonymous reviewers. Errors and omissions are the sole responsibility of the authors.

Cambridge Elements ⁼

Contentious Politics

David S. Meyer
University of California, Irvine

David S. Meyer is Professor of Sociology and Political Science at the University of California, Irvine. He has written extensively on social movements and public policy, mostly in the United States, and is a winner of the John D. McCarthy Award for Lifetime Achievement in the Scholarship of Social Movements and Collective Behavior.

Suzanne Staggenborg
University of Pittsburgh

Suzanne Staggenborg is Professor of Sociology at the University of Pittsburgh. She has studied organizational and political dynamics in a variety of social movements, including the women's movement and the environmental movement, and is a winner of the John D. McCarthy Award for Lifetime Achievement in the Scholarship of Social Movements and Collective Behavior.

About the Series

Cambridge Elements series in Contentious Politics provides an important opportunity to bridge research and communication about the politics of protest across disciplines and between the academy and a broader public. Our focus is on political engagement, disruption, and collective action that extends beyond the boundaries of conventional institutional politics. Social movements, revolutionary campaigns, organized reform efforts, and more or less spontaneous uprisings are the important and interesting developments that animate contemporary politics; we welcome studies and analyses that promote better understanding and dialogue.

Cambridge Elements ☰

Contentious Politics

Printed in the United States
by Baker & Taylor Publisher Services